The Diffusion of Public and Private Sustainability Regulations

The Diffusion of Public and Private Sustainability Regulations

The Responses of Follower Countries

Edited by

Etsuyo Michida

Senior Research Fellow, Institute of Developing Economies, JETRO, Japan

John Humphrey

Honorary Visiting Professor, Department of Strategy and Marketing, University of Sussex Business School, Brighton, UK

David Vogel

Professor Emeritus, Haas School of Business, Department of Political Science, University of California, Berkeley, USA

INSTITUTE OF DEVELOPING ECONOMIES (IDE), JETRO

Cheltenham, UK • Northampton, MA, USA

Published by
Edward Elgar Publishing Limited
The Lypiatts
15 Lansdown Road
Cheltenham
Glos GL50 2JA
UK

Edward Elgar Publishing, Inc.
William Pratt House
9 Dewey Court
Northampton
Massachusetts 01060
USA

A catalogue record for this book
is available from the British Library

Library of Congress Control Number: 2020952046

This book is available electronically in the **Elgar**online
Political Science and Public Policy subject collection
http://dx.doi.org/10.4337/9781800880948

ISBN 978 1 80088 093 1 (cased)
ISBN 978 1 80088 094 8 (eBook)

Printed and bound by CPI Group (UK) Ltd, Croydon, CR0 4YY

Contents

Figures and tables

FIGURES

TABLES

Contributors

Fang-Ting Cheng is Research Fellow, Institute of Developing Economies, JETRO.

John Humphrey is Honorary Visiting Professor, University of Sussex Business School.

Hajime Iseda is Sustainable Design Manager, Sustainable Design & Consulting Group, Advanced Design Department, Design Department Head Office, Takenaka Corporation.

Michikazu Kojima is Senior Economist, Economic Research Institute for ASEAN and East Asia.

Etsuyo Michida is Senior Research Fellow, Institute of Developing Economies, JETRO.

Kenji Shiraishi is Researcher, Renewable and Appropriate Energy Laboratory, University of California, Berkeley.

David Vogel is Professor Emeritus, Haas School of Business, Department of Political Science, University of California, Berkeley.

Akiko Yanai is Senior Research Fellow, Institute of Developing Economies, JETRO.

1. Introduction to *The Diffusion of Public and Private Sustainability Regulations: The Responses of Follower Countries*

Etsuyo Michida, John Humphrey and David Vogel

This collection of chapters focuses on the spread of environmental and food safety regulations to Asia and Africa. One of the striking features of the global economy over the past 20–30 years has been the rapid spread of such regulations across jurisdictions. International treaties are one way in which regulations and policies can spread across countries, and in the environmental field initiatives such as the Montréal Protocol controlling emissions of chlorofluorocarbons (CFCs) and the Minamata Convention on Mercury (Meckling, 2018) have been promoted in this way. Nevertheless, much of the cross-national spread of environmental policies has taken place in the absence of such organized international action. Tews and Busch argue that "global convergence of environmental policy can take place in the absence of a strong international regime, within which states committed themselves to certain policies and which provides strong compliance mechanisms" (2001: 168).

The spread of policies through such mechanisms is called "policy diffusion." This has been defined as "the process by which policy innovations are communicated in the international system and adopted voluntarily by an increasing number of countries over time" (Busch, Jörgens and Tews, 2005: 149). The extensive literature in this field analyzes not only the spread of environmental policies, but also issues such as employment and welfare policies (Dolowitz and Marsh, 2000), the adoption of anti-smoking initiatives by US cities (Shipan and Volden, 2008), the global spread of controls over the production and use of chemicals (Biedenkopf, 2012; Michida, 2014), the adoption of performance management systems in Chinese cities (Liu and Li, 2016) and the way in which European Union (EU) institutions and policies have been adopted in countries and regions far from the EU's immediate zone of influence (Börzel and Risse, 2012). This literature focuses on a range of policy diffusion issues, and two of these are particularly salient for the chapters in this volume. The first concerns the motivations for diffusion. What are the factors that induce authorities in one jurisdiction to adopt policies developed in another? The second is about policy convergence and divergence. Policies and policy ideas may spread (or diffuse), but the result is not necessarily the implementation of identical policies across locations (Gilardi, 2013). Domestic factors may influence how policies are implemented, and while policy principles may be adopted, the design and implementation of concrete policies may differ.

The chapters in this volume explore these issues but add to the literature in two ways. The first is geographical focus. While much of the existing literature has addressed policy diffusion among Northern countries that share similar norms, policy priorities and stages of development (Busch, Jörgens and Tews, 2005; Héritier, Knill and Mingers, 1996), this volume focuses on non-Western countries (both developed and developing) in their role as follower countries that adopt food safety, environmental and sustainability policies, but under conditions different to those of the originating country. Compared to the rich literatures on Europe and the United States, limited research has been undertaken in non-Western countries. Developing country cases, where they exist, are largely addressed as samples of a larger set of countries (Busch, Jörgens and Tews, 2005; Simmons and Elkins, 2004). Research focusing on the diffusion of European environmental policy to Asian developing countries (Biedenkopf, 2012; Michida, 2017) shows that the motivations for adopting regulations or standards developed in other jurisdictions and the extent of their divergence reflect a variety of local conditions, including a country's social and economic priorities, the capacity of the state to implement policy mechanisms, the interaction with existing laws and regulations, the capabilities of local producers and consumer preferences.

The second contribution of this volume lies in its attention to the role of non-state actors in the cross-national diffusion of policies relating to the environment and food safety. The literature on policy diffusion focuses predominantly on government-to-government policy spread. For example, Shipan and Volden characterize policy diffusion as "the spread of [policy] innovations from one government to another" (2008: 841). Simmons, Dobbin and Garrett also confine the discussion to government policy: "International policy diffusion occurs when government policy decisions in a given country are systematically conditioned by prior policy choices made in other countries" (2006: 787).

This focus on government policymaking has occurred at a time when a salient feature of transnational governance has been the rapid growth of non-state forms of transnational regulation. A large number of "private" transnational governance initiatives around the environment, sustainability and food safety have emerged since the 1990s, and it has been argued that

"An increasing portion of business regulation emanates not from conventional state and interstate institutions, but from an array of private sector, civil society, multi-stakeholder and hybrid public–private institutions operating in a dynamic, transnational regulatory space" (Eberlein et al., 2014: 1). Initiatives include the Marine Stewardship Council and Forest Stewardship Council sustainability standards (Bush and Oosterveer, 2015; Dingwerth, 2008; Pattberg, 2005), Roundtables for the sustainable production of commodities such as soy, palm oil, sugar and biofuels (Hospes, 2014; Schouten and Glasbergen, 2011), and "green" building design (Schindler, 2010). These initiatives, which have been developed predominantly through the activities of multi-stakeholder coalitions led by businesses and non-governmental organizations (NGOs) from high-income countries, are designed to control the way in which products are made so that desirable impacts relating to food safety, social conditions and environmental consequences are achieved, or undesirable impacts eliminated or mitigated. These form part of the global diffusion of policies in this area.[1]

The next section of this Introduction develops a discussion of the diffusion of public and private regulations, paying particular attention to the relationship between the motivations for diffusion and the degree of convergence between regulations in the countries of origin and those in countries to which they have diffused. Section 1.2 then discusses the chapters in the volume and identifies their contributions to the discussion of the diffusion of public and private regulations. Section 1.3 concludes.

1.1   POLICY DIFFUSION: MOTIVATIONS AND CONVERGENCE

The literature on policy diffusion has highlighted four classes of mechanisms that might drive the diffusion of policies across countries: learning, emulation, competition and coercion (Gilardi, 2013; Shipan and Volden, 2008; Simmons and Elkins, 2004).[2] These can be taken as a continuum that ranges from purely voluntary action to adopt a standard through to adoption as a result of an exercise of coercive power (Dolowitz and Marsh, 2000: 9), with diffusion often arising from a combination of these mechanisms. While the discussion of these factors has been confined to the adoption of public policies by public agencies, it will be argued that they also apply to the diffusion of private regulations.

Learning and emulation are at the voluntary end of the continuum. Learning refers to the process by which policy diffusion is prompted by the examination of the experiences of other countries (or jurisdictions) and the use of this knowledge to inform choices about policy adoption. One example of learning within Asia was the introduction across the region of bans on the import of waste plastic for recycling. This policy was first introduced in China at the end of 2017, but neighboring Asian countries subsequently introduced similar bans, partly because of learning from China, and partly in order to manage inflows of waste diverted to them following the change of Chinese policy. Transnational networks of policymakers often promote such learning and diffusion, as discussed in the case of municipal climate strategies in Europe (Hakelberg, 2014). Learning from the experience of others simplifies policy choices. It acts as an important mechanism for the development of local regulations by both government and business.

In the case of learning, the focus is on the policy being adopted. Emulation, in contrast, arises when the motivation for transfer is not the policy (or the action), but rather the characteristics of the actors that had previously adopted it (Shipan and Volden, 2008: 842–3). According to Biedenkopf, "Emulation is the mechanism by which policy makers adopt policy similar to that of another jurisdiction based on the belief that this policy is legitimate and appropriate" (2012: 481). While some analysts have emphasized the importance of geographical proximity in the operation of the emulation mechanism (Howlett, 2000), cases involving geographical distance have also been discussed. For example, it has been argued that the EU's development of its own institutions influenced the characteristics of the ASEAN Charter and the Andean Court of Justice through a process of emulation (Börzel and Risse, 2012: 2–3). As the diffusion of particular policies becomes more widespread, so the legitimacy and appropriateness of these policies becomes established. Countries may adopt policies because this shows that they are ready to work within a framework of widely accepted international rules. Both learning and emulation are associated with the voluntary adoption of policies developed in other jurisdictions.

The competition motivation relates to the way in which policies might spread because countries seek to maintain their competitiveness. This can lead to two types of diffusion. The first is across countries that occupy similar positions within the world economy. If one country adopts a policy that provides it with a competitive advantage (for example, a more favorable tax regime for foreign investors, or the provision of better infrastructure and support facilities) then other countries might adopt similar policies in order not to be disadvantaged as an investment location (Oman, 2000).

The second type of competition-driven diffusion occurs when policies are adopted in order to conform to public or private regulations required for access to destination markets. Such requirements are often introduced into preferential trade agreements, as discussed by Hafner-Burton (2005), who examines how such agreements can be used to change exporting country behavior in areas such as human rights and child labor. Similar market access conditionalities are used to promote the diffusion of environmental policies. This is seen clearly in the case of the EU's controls over the timber trade. The EU Timber Regulation requires companies placing timber on the EU market to establish that it has been harvested in accordance with the laws of the exporting country, and the EU provides guidance about how this might be done (European Commission, 2016). At the same time, Voluntary Partnership Agreements with timber-exporting countries redefine the definition of what counts as legally-harvested product and commit the partner countries to introduce controls not only over timber exported to the EU, but also that placed on the domestic market of the exporting country or exported to any other country (Humphrey, 2017: 33–7).

The use of market access as a lever to change policy in exporting countries can be implemented in different ways. One option is to require the exporting country to introduce domestic regulations that will regulate behavior to achieve the desired goals. The regulations do not have to be the same as those adopted in importing countries: it is merely necessary for new regulations to have an equivalent outcome in terms of the desired goals. Thus, the EU Food and Veterinary Office checks the food safety systems of countries exporting to the EU to verify that they have the capacity to regulate the food export businesses in ways that provide a level of assurance equivalent to that achieved by food safety systems within the EU (Humphrey, 2017). Where there are known and unresolved problems with imported products, additional border checks may be required on entry, or policy innovations required in the exporting country that will provide assurances about the acceptability of exported products. The negotiation between the EU and China about controls over aflatoxin contamination in Chinese groundnut exports would be an example (Diaz Rios and Jaffee, 2008: 19–20). Finally, governments in exporting countries may incorporate export market requirements into domestic law in order to create convergence between domestic and export market regulations and reduce the burdens placed on exporters. Export businesses, including multinational companies, may lobby governments to take such measures (Vogel, 1995).

However, as the consequences of non-adoption become more severe, so the motivating factor looks closer to coercion, as outlined by Dolowitz and Marsh (2000). The extreme case of coercion identified in the diffusion literature is where there is a direct and hierarchical exercise of coercive power by one government body over another. Liu and Li give the example of one level of government in China exerting direct control over the adoption of policies by another, subordinate level. They argue that this should not be considered a case of policy diffusion at all, with the result that they restrict diffusion mechanisms to competition, learning and imitation (Liu and Li, 2016: 633). Other authors take a different view, arguing that powerful actors in the global economy can influence policy in other countries and that this should be considered as diffusion through coercion. Drezner defines coercion as "the threat or act by a sender government or governments to disrupt economic exchange with the target state, unless the target acquiesces to an articulated demand" (2003:

643).[3] Dobbin, Simmons and Garrett provide examples of coercive diffusion driven by governments and international organizations:

> Coercion can be exercised by governments, international organizations, and non-governmental actors through physical force ... the manipulation of economic costs and benefits, and even the monopolization of information or expertise. Thus, the preferences of the U.S. government, the European Union (EU), the International Monetary Fund (IMF), and the World Bank may shape policy in countries reliant on those entities for trade, foreign direct investment, aid, grants, loans, or security. Some argue that coercion is not a mechanism of diffusion, in that policy change is not voluntary. We do not treat military force as a mechanism of policy diffusion, but we do review studies of persuasion, loan and aid conditionality, and unilateral policy choices that shape the choices of other countries. (Dobbin, Simmons and Garrett, 2007: 454)

Such coercion has been associated with what Vogel (1995) terms the "race-to-the-top." Regulatory adoption leads to upwards convergence of regulations.

These same diffusion mechanisms are visible in the spread of private regulation. The proliferation of private standards occurs, in part, as a result of learning and emulation. Standard-setting bodies learn from each other, both informally and through networks of standard-setting bodies, including the ISO and organizations such as the International Federation of Organic Agriculture Movements (IFOAM), the ISEAL Alliance, whose Board of Directors includes representatives from many private standard-setting organizations that develop and administer private standards (ISEAL Alliance, 2018: 10), and business groups such as the Consumer Goods Forum, which is responsible for the benchmarking of standards through the Global Food Safety Initiative.

The competition mechanism for the diffusion of policies aimed at regulating the behavior of businesses in supply chains is central to non-state, market-driven (NSMD) standards. Even without state authority, such private regulation is able to create positive and negative sanctions to shape behavior. Cashore refers to:

> the emergence of domestic and transnational private governance systems that derive their policy-making authority not from the state, but from the manipulation of global markets and attention to customer preferences ... nongovernmental organizations (NGOs) have developed governance structures and social and environmentally focused rules concerning the production and sale of products and services. (Cashore, 2002: 503–4)

Prakash and Potoski provide a clear example of the effect of trade in promoting the diffusion of private regulation. They studied levels of certification for the ISO 14001 environmental management standard across a panel of 108 countries over a seven-year period.[4] The key finding is that levels of certification are not related to the overall trade exposure of a country (exports in relation to gross domestic product, GDP), but rather to the levels of certification in the countries to which the country is exporting:

> Our results suggest that while high levels of trade per se may not significantly affect firms' decisions to adopt ISO 14001, trade can be a vehicle to disseminate ISO 14001 if the key export markets have widely adopted this nongovernmental regulation. Thus, importing countries are influencing organizational practices in the exporting countries, not vice-versa. (Prakash and Potoski, 2006: 359)

The case where exporting businesses find that certain customers make ISO 14001 certification an order-qualifying criterion is a clear example of the competition motivation. To the extent that exporters are free to target different customers and different markets or may find other ways of displaying their environmental credentials to potential customers, this is not coercion. However, the pressure to adopt standards may be very strong. For example, Kenya's exports of fresh vegetables have mostly been directed to the UK and Dutch markets, and exporters have invested in facilities that meet the specific requirements of these countries in terms of compliance to both public and private regulations and the provision of services such as food preparation and the use of customer-specific packaging. These represent upfront investments whose value would be considerably reduced if used for preparing exports to other countries or market niches (Humphrey, 2008). In such circumstances, businesses are under pressure to comply with the rules set out by the standard, although it is also possible for local variants of the standard, benchmarked to the transnational standard, to provide some local adaptation while offering equivalent outcomes.

The comparison between coercion-competition and learning-emulation factors creates an apparently simple contrast. If the adoption of regulations is driven by the desire to maintain access to particular export markets, equivalence must be maintained between what is adopted in the exporting country and the requirements of the destination market. Trading relations provide motivations for regulatory alignment. If, on the other hand, there are no direct trading relationships to drive alignment, countries are more likely to be motivated by learning and emulation and to adjust policy selection and policy implementation to a greater extent to meet the requirements of the domestic economy and existing regulatory frameworks.

The chapters in this volume that focus on trade-related standards (relating to food safety in fishing and palm oil standards) show that while strong trading links drive the diffusion of policy and the alignment of standards, the outcome is not always a strong policy alignment. Differences in priorities and capabilities may make it difficult to achieve full alignment. Equally, the chapters that focus on regulations not directly relating to trade (building standards, energy efficiency and emissions trading schemes) demonstrate how, even in the absence of trading relationships, pressure for standards alignment may exist. In particular, new standards created through learning and emulation may face design and implementation constraints arising from the need to interact with standards in other jurisdictions. These points are developed further in the discussion of each of the chapters.

1.2   CHAPTER CONTENTS AND FINDINGS

The clearest example of a strong association between trade linkages and regulatory alignment is found in Chapter 4 by Yanai on fisheries policies in Tanzania, Madagascar and Mauritius. It focuses specifically on the issue of food safety regulations and discusses the role of the competition and coercion mechanisms for diffusion through an analysis of how these countries responded to the regulatory framework implemented in one significant export market, the EU. The chapter outlines the particular stringency of EU regulations as they apply to food of animal origin and provides an account of how the EU monitors exporting country compliance to its regulations by means of audits that cover legislation, the activities of the competent authorities for food safety and the implementation of controls by food business operators. It then examines how the three exporting countries responded to the EU food hygiene regulations introduced in 2004. While all three countries changed their laws and regulations in response to the new hygiene regulations, the chapter argues that the speed of response varied across the three countries and that Tanzania was noticeably slower in introducing changes than either Madagascar or Mauritius.

The chapter provides two explanations for this difference. The first relates to the importance of the EU fish products market for the three economies. The more important the market, the greater the pressure for compliance and the diffusion of regulatory policies from Europe to the exporting countries. In other words, different countries lie at different points along the continuum from competition to coercion. It is argued that the determining factor is not solely the share of the EU market in a country's total exports of fish and fish products, but rather relates to the importance of fish production and export for the economy as a whole. While the EU only accounts for one third of fish exports from Mauritius, the fishing industry as a whole is much more significant for Mauritius than for the other two countries, and this drives harmonization. In addition to this, the chapter points to the consequences for each of the three countries of their position within Regional Economic Communities in Africa. In this respect, Tanzania's membership of the East African Community is particularly relevant, because this grouping has advanced further than other regional groupings in terms of harmonization of standards, including for fish. This means that the process of revising regulations in response to the requirements of the EU market involves regional agreements and consent, which reduces the speed of responses to changes in EU regulations.

Chapter 2 by Humphrey and Michida examines the drivers of the development of national standards for sustainable palm oil in Indonesia and Malaysia. Prior to the introduction of the Indonesia Sustainable Palm Oil (ISPO) and Malaysian Sustainable Palm Oil (MSPO) standards, the main certification scheme for establishing the sustainability of palm oil production was the Roundtable on Sustainable Palm Oil (RSPO). This is an NSMD standard developed by a multi-stakeholder coalition that is accepted widely in Europe (by public authorities and businesses) as a key indicator of sustainability. Indonesia and Malaysia are the world's largest palm oil producers and are responsible for 90% of global exports, and the decision to create national standards that diverge from the RSPO standard—particularly in the areas of Free, Prior and Informed Consent and the protection of land with High Conservation Values—has been interpreted in much of the literature as an attempt to construct rivals to the RSPO that are designed to weaken environmental and community protections and prioritize producer interests and economic growth. In other words, national governments are trying to change the premises of the debate on sustainability.

Chapter 2 challenges this view. It shows that the declining importance of Europe as a destination market compared to the rapidly growing demand for palm oil in Asia opens up the possibility of creating alternative standards that might be acceptable in these newer markets. However, evidence is provided to show that the largest destination markets in Asia have very weak demand for certified sustainable palm oil of any type. In this context, it is argued that the drivers of the two national standards have become largely domestic, rather than linked to export markets. In particular, the two distinctive characteristics of these national standards—they have become mandatory for all producers, and thus extended to include smallholder farmers—not only significantly extend their scope as drivers of sustainability, given the importance of small farmer palm oil production in both countries, but also transform the standards into drivers of rural transformation. To be implemented effectively, they require extensive programs of rural development, smallholder capability-building and the development of group certification schemes. Accordingly, ambitious programs have been introduced in both countries to certify all smallholder farmer production. However, the chapter casts doubt on the ability of governments in both countries, and particularly in Indonesia, with respect to both the ability to transform smallholder farmer production and the capacity of the schemes to monitor and enforce the rules they set down. In both cases, it is too early to judge their success.

Chapters 2 and 4 are both concerned with trade-related standards. The other three chapters focus on standards developed primarily for the domestic market that are diffused through the learning and emulation mechanisms. Chapter 3 by Shiraishi and Iseda focuses on the adoption of standards aimed at reducing the environmental impact of the construction and operation of buildings (green building standards). The building sector is one of the largest contributors to greenhouse gas (GHG) emissions and primary energy consumption, and developing standards for economically, environmentally and socially sustainable buildings is increasing across the world. In this field, there has been a proliferation of local standards, with the chapter identifying 21 different standards developed across 26 countries.

The core questions of this chapter are first, whether it is cost-effective to create green building rating systems that respond to the specific conditions in a particular country in the context of a globalized market economy; and second, the relationship between domestic and global rating systems. These issues are explored through a quantitative analysis of levels of certification to Leadership in Energy and Environmental Design (LEED), the dominant global green building standard, and how levels of LEED certification are affected by the development of domestic green building standards. More in-depth analysis of interactions between standards is provided through an analysis of three green building standards: the Building Research Establishment Environmental Assessment Method (BREEAM), developed in the UK; the Comprehensive Assessment System for Building Environmental Efficiency (CASBEE) standard developed in Japan; and the Australian Green Star standard. The development of domestic systems facilitates take-up because they can be designed to be better suited to domestic conditions and domestic regulatory frameworks.

The quantitative analysis shows that, overall, the development of alternative local standards for green construction within a given country reduces the number of companies certified to LEED. More detailed examination of the relationship between LEED and the national standards developed in Australia, Japan and the UK shows that while the national standards in Japan and Australia have a statistically significant negative impact on levels of LEED certification in the two countries, the same does not apply for the UK. This is explained by a stronger convergence between the UK standard and LEED, which has a higher level of uptake in the UK. It is argued that while the development of local systems facilitates take-up because of their better fit with local needs, there is a resulting trade-off because local adaptation increases the divergences between the local standards and the globally accepted standard, and this drives up costs and makes local businesses that use them less competitive in global markets. The greater the convergence between the global and local standards, the easier it is for businesses to acquire certification to both standards and be able to expand into global markets.

Chapter 5 by Cheng examines emission trading schemes (ETSs) for GHGs in China, Korea and Japan. ETSs have been adopted across many countries and emulation and imitation are the main drivers of diffusion. Carbon market policy instruments cannot be simply copied from one jurisdiction to another, and as a result many ETSs have been modified to fit location-specific political, economic, social and institutional contexts. This creates considerable difficulties in integrating ETS markets, and yet in spite of this countries continue to engage in dialogue about ETSs and continue to search for common carbon pricing mechanisms. This leads to the core question of this chapter, "What motivates East Asian countries to continue multilateral conversations and to cooperate by sharing each other's experiences in spite of the difficulties in integrating different ETS systems?"

As has been seen in other chapters, policy diffusion does not necessarily mean "copying" or "policy convergence." In the case of ETSs, regulations are altered to meet the needs of diverse stakeholders and a range of local conditions. It is evident that in the three countries a considerable amount of experimentation and learning has taken place in the process of introducing ETSs. The three countries all engaged in a phased introduction process, with schemes introduced in phases or a succession of schemes introduced as local learning increased. Alongside "diffusion through learning" there was also a process of "learning after diffusion." This allowed experience to be accumulated and implementation problems and market failures to be addressed, but at the expense of increasing incompatibility between national schemes. These vary with respect to emission reduction targets, the range of sectors covered, their compliance mechanisms and the types of gases that they cover. As a result, it becomes very hard for emissions credits to be traded across national borders, or between ETSs.

In spite of these differences and non-compatibilities, cooperation between schemes continues. One reason for this is that the schemes can learn from each other, creating trust and preparing the ground for possible future cooperation. Such learning can improve schemes in general, and also enable countries to learn how to improve their specific domestic systems. A second reason is that many organizations and policy communities, both regional and global, facilitate exchanges with a view to promoting cooperation. The chapter provides a detailed analysis of the different activities and policy communities that support these knowledge exchanges. Nevertheless, these activities are more focused on improving each national system than creating the conditions for ETS integration. This case illustrates both the difficulties of linking different domestic initiatives once local conditions and local learning have led to differentiation between them, while at the same time showing that there is continuing interaction and learning between the schemes.

Chapter 6 by Kojima examines energy efficiency policy in Asia. Studies of policy diffusion have examined the factors that lead to policy divergence in the process of policy diffusion. This is often explained by reference to the specificity of domestic forces and domestic capabilities. This chapter notes a considerable heterogeneity in the timing and content of energy efficiency policy programs across 11 Asian countries. It then analyses some of the factors leading to the observed differences in timing and content, paying particular attention to the role of energy intensity and energy self-sufficiency in shaping policies in the period up to the beginning of the 21st century. It adds to this, however, by introducing a temporal dimension, stressing how the motivations behind the adoption of energy efficiency policies have changed over time from responding to higher energy prices to recognizing the imperative of reducing GHG emissions.

The early adopters of energy efficiency policies in Asia were motivated by oil price rises, but their responses varied according to their energy intensity and energy self-reliance. Energy intensive economies have a greater incentive to introduce energy efficiency policies, while countries that are more self-sufficient in energy have fewer incentives to do so. These factors explain some of the differentiation in policy responses at this time. By the 1990s, however, GHG emissions and mitigation efforts were a much more significant driver of energy efficiency policies. At this time, countries that were relatively energy sufficient were still laggards, but after 2005 there was a much more general adoption of energy efficiency policies, with even energy-rich countries enacting energy efficiency regulations.

1.3   CONCLUSIONS

This volume examines five cases of the diffusion of public and private regulations. These confirm that trade-related motivations are one driving force for regulatory transfer. The continuing importance of the RSPO for access to the European market (Chapter 2) and the impact of EU regulations on fisheries policy in Africa (Chapter 4) highlight the continuing importance of competition as a mechanism for policy diffusion that operates across both public and private regulation. Exporting countries have to take into account the regulatory environment in destination markets, but they do not necessarily respond passively to these challenges. The case of national palm oil standards shows that the shifting balance of power in the global economy opens up new opportunities. Demand from non-Western countries, which grew rapidly in the first two decades of the 21st century, has changed some of the power dynamics around public and private regulation. At the same time, countries such as Malaysia and Indonesia (and Brazil) have become more confident about creating standards rather than passively accepting existing regulatory frameworks. The growth of nationalist sentiment in the global economy may reinforce this tendency. The two cases also show that responses to public and private regulations in destination markets may be shaped by domestic factors, and this was particularly evident in the case of the national palm oil standards in Indonesia and Malaysia.

The cases of green building standards, ETSs and energy efficiency policies fall in the terrain of learning and emulation as diffusion mechanisms. These are not related to trade, although there may be trade-related impacts, as would be the case with respect to international trade in building design and services. In this case, the studies show that the process of diffusion is far from limited to the introduction of policies developed in other jurisdictions with some greater or lesser degree of adaptation to local conditions. In all three cases, there is a considerable degree of interaction between national policies and the extra-national environment. The ETS case study shows ongoing interactions between different adopters and learning across jurisdictions, allowing experimentation that had the potentially unintended consequence of hampering cross-national integration. The green building case study points to the proliferation of green building standards and their adaptation to local circumstances, but also to the downside of divergence. In the case of energy efficiency policies, different motivations and different drivers of change led to a heterogeneous landscaper policy diffusion across Asia.

Global integration drives policy diffusion, trade-related regulations are powerful drivers of policy diffusion through the mechanisms of competition and coercion, and the increasing integration of the global economy facilitates emulation and learning. Public and private policies and regulations have spread across countries, and the trend is likely to continue. Nevertheless, the global economy is itself changing with the growth of emerging economies and the rise of nationalist sentiment in some developed and emerging economies. Follower countries may become more proactive and innovative in their responses to regulatory environments, but the studies in this collection show that there are a variety of ways in which choices and consequences are shaped by the external environment, and further work is required on how countries respond to the new challenges that they face, the resources they have available to do this and the linkages and interactions that both facilitate and constrain their actions.

NOTES

1. These non-state governance forms have been referred to variously as private standards, non-state market-driven standards (Cashore et al., 2007), civil regulation (Vogel, 2010; Zadek and Forstater, 1999), private regulation (Cafaggi, 2010) and private law (van der Meulen, 2011). This chapter uses the terms private regulation and public regulation to distinguish between state and non-state governance mechanisms.
2. Sometimes "imitation" rather than "emulation" is presented as the fourth category (for example, Hakelberg, 2014; Shipan and Volden, 2008), but the mechanisms described are much the same.
3. Cited by Hafner-Burton (2005: 599).
4. The International Organisation for Standardization (ISO) is described by Prakash and Potoski as a non-state body because its members are "private sector national bodies," such as the American National Standards Institute and the Deutsches Institut für Normung (Prakash and Potoski, 2006: 352).

REFERENCES

Biedenkopf, K. (2012). Hazardous substances in electronics: The effect of European Union risk regulation on China. *European Journal of Risk Regulation* 3(4), 477–88, doi 10.1017/S1867299X00002415.

Börzel, T.A. and Risse, T. (2012). From Europeanisation to diffusion: Introduction. *West European Politics* 35(1), 1–19, doi 10.1080/01402382.2012.631310.

Busch, P.-O., Jörgens, H. and Tews, K. (2005). The global diffusion of regulatory instruments: The making of a new international environmental regime. *Annals of the American Academy of Political and Social Science* 598(1), 146–67, doi 10.1177/0002716204272355.

Bush, S.R. and Oosterveer, P. (2015). Vertically differentiating environmental standards: The case of the Marine Stewardship Council. *Sustainability* 7, 1861–83, doi 10.3390/su7021861.

Cafaggi, F. (2010). Private regulation, supply chain and contractual networks. Paper presented at the VIII Annual Conference of the Euro-Latin Study Network on Integration and Trade, Paris, October.

Cashore, B. (2002). Legitimacy and the privatization of environmental governance: How non-state market-driven (NSMD) governance systems gain rule-making authority. *Governance: An International Journal of Policy, Administration, and Institutions* 15(4), 503–29, doi 10.1111/1468–0491.00199.

Cashore, B., Auld, G., Bernstein, S. and McDermott, C. (2007). Can non-state governance "ratchet up" global environmental standards? Lessons from the forest sector. *Review of European Comparative & International Environmental Law* 16(2), 158–72, doi 10.1111/j.1467–9388.2007.00560.x.

Diaz Rios, L. and Jaffee, S. (2008). Barrier, catalyst, or distraction? Standards, competitiveness, and Africa's groundnut exports to Europe. Agricultural and Rural Development Discussion Paper, 39. Washington, DC: World Bank. Retrieved from http://siteresources.worldbank.org/INTARD/Resources/Making_the_Grade_ePDF2 .pdf (last accessed July 2018).

Dingwerth, K. (2008). North-South parity in global governance: The affirmative procedures of the Forest Stewardship Council. *Global Governance* 14(1), 53–71.

Dobbin, F., Simmons, B. and Garrett, G. (2007). The global diffusion of public policies: Social construction, coercion, competition, or learning? *Annual Review of Sociology* 33, 449–72, doi 10.1146/annurev.soc.33.090106.142507.

Dolowitz, D.P. and Marsh, D. (2000). Learning from abroad: The role of policy transfer in contemporary policy-making. *Governance: An International Journal of Policy, Administration, and Institutions* 13(1), 5–23, doi 10.1111/0952–1895.00121.

Drezner, D.W. (2003). The hidden hand of economic coercion. *International Organization* 57(3), 643–59, doi 10.1017/S0020818303573052.

Eberlein, G.B., Abbott, K., Black, J., Meidinger, E. and Wood, S. (2014). Transnational business governance interactions: Conceptualization and framework for analysis. *Regulation & Governance* 8(1), 1–21, doi 10.1111/rego.12030.

European Commission (2016). Guidance document for the EU timber regulation. Commission Notice of 12.2.2016. C(2016) 755 final. Retrieved from https://www.agriculture.gov.ie/media/migration/forestry/eutr/EUTRCommi ssionGuidanceFeb2016160216.pdf (last accessed April 2014).

Gilardi, F. (2013). Transnational diffusion: Norms, ideas, and policies. In W. Carlsnaes, T. Risse and B.A. Simmons (eds), *Handbook of International Relations*. London: Sage, pp. 453–77.

Hafner-Burton, E.M. (2005). Trading human rights: How preferential trade agreements influence government repression. *International Organization* 59(3), 593–629.

Hakelberg, L. (2014). Governance by diffusion: Transnational municipal networks and the spread of local climate strategies in Europe. *Global Environmental Politics* 14(1), 107–29, doi 10.1162/GLEP_a_00216.

Héritier, A., Knill, C. and Mingers, S. (1996). *Ringing the Changes in Europe: Regulatory Competition and the Transformation of the State. Britain, France, Germany.* Berlin and New York: Walter de Gruyter.

Hospes, O. (2014). Marking the success or end of global multi-stakeholder governance? The rise of national sustainability standards in Indonesia and Brazil for palm oil and soy. *Agriculture and Human Values* 31(3), 425–37, doi 10.1007/s10460–014–9511–9.

Howlett, M. (2000). Beyond legalism? Policy ideas, implementation styles and emulation-based convergence in Canadian and US environmental policy. *Journal of Public Policy* 20(3), 305–29, doi 10.1017/S0143814X00000866.

Humphrey, J. (2008). Private standards, small farmers and donor policy: EUREPGAP in Kenya. IDS Working Paper, 308. Brighton: Institute of Development Studies. Retrieved from http://www.ids.ac.uk/files/Wp308.pdf (last accessed June 2018).

Humphrey, J. (2017). Regulation, standards, and risk management in the context of globalisation. In E. Michida, J. Humphrey and K. Nabeshima (eds), *Regulations and International Trade: New Sustainability Challenges for East Asia*. Basingstoke: Palgrave Macmillan, pp. 21–58.

ISEAL Alliance (2018). Understanding certified small producers' needs. London: ISEAL Alliance. Retrieved from https://www.isealalliance.org/sites/default/files/resource/2018–07/ISEAL_Producer_Needs_Report_2018_0.pdf (last accessed January 2020).

Liu, W. and Li, W. (2016). Divergence and convergence in the diffusion of performance management in China. *Public Performance & Management Review* 39(3), 630–54, doi 10.1080/15309576.2015.1138060.

Meckling, J. (2018). The developmental state in global regulation: Economic change and climate policy. *European Journal of International Relations* 24(1), 58–81, doi 10.1177/1354066117700966.

Michida, E. (2014). The policy impact of product-related environmental regulations in Asia. IDE Discussion Paper, 451. Chiba: Institute of Developing Economies.

Michida, E. (2017). Regulatory diffusion from Europe to Asia. In E. Michida, J. Humphrey and K. Nabeshima (eds), *Regulations and International Trade: New Sustainability Challenges for East Asia*. Basingstoke: Palgrave Macmillan, pp. 59–84.

Oman, C. (2000). Policy competition for foreign direct investment: A study of competition among governments to attract FDI. Development Centre Studies. Paris: OECD Development Centre. Retrieved from http://www.oecd.org/mena/competitiveness/35275189.pdf (last accessed January 2020).

Pattberg, P. (2005). The Forest Stewardship Council: Risk and potential of private forest governance. *The Journal of Environment and Development* 14, 356–74.

Prakash, A. and Potoski, M. (2006). Racing to the bottom? Trade, environmental governance, and ISO 14001. *American Journal of Political Sciences* 50(2), 350–64.

Schindler, S.B. (2010). Following industry's LEED: Municipal adoption of private green building standards. *Florida Law Review* 62(2), 285–350.

Schouten, G. and Glasbergen, P. (2011). Creating legitimacy in global private governance: The case of the Roundtable on Sustainable Palm Oil. *Ecological Economics* 70(11), 1891–99, doi 10.1016/j.ecolecon.2011.03.012.

Shipan, C.R. and Volden, C. (2008). The mechanisms of policy diffusion. *American Journal of Political Sciences* 52(4), 840–57.

Simmons, B.A. and Elkins, Z. (2004). The globalization of liberalization: Policy diffusion in the international political economy. *American Political Science Review* 98(1), 171–89.

Simmons, B.A., Dobbin, F. and Garrett, G. (2006). Introduction: The international diffusion of liberalism. *International Organisation* 60(4), 781–810, doi 10.1017/S0020818306060267.

Tews, K. and Busch, P.-O. (2001). Governance by diffusion? Potentials and restrictions of environmental policy diffusion. In F. Biermann, R. Brohm and K. Dingwerth (eds), *Berlin Conference on the Human Dimensions of Global Environmental Change*. Berlin: Potsdam Institute for Climate Impact Research (PIK), pp. 168–82.

van der Meulen, B. (2011). Private food law: The emergence of a concept. In B. van der Meulen (ed.), *Private Food Law*. Wageningen: Wageningen Academic Publishers, pp. 29–50.

Vogel, D. (1995). *Trading Up: Consumer and Environmental Regulation in a Global Economy*. Cambridge MA: MIT Press.

Vogel, D. (2010). The private regulation of global corporate conduct: Achievements and limitations. *Business & Society* 49(1), 68–87, doi 10.1177/0007650309343407.

Zadek, S. and Forstater, M. (1999). Making civil regulation work. In M.K. Addo (ed.), *Human Rights and the Responsibilities of Transnational Corporations*. The Hague: Kluwer Law International, pp. 69–76.

2. National palm oil standards in Asia: motivations and impacts on trade and rural development

John Humphrey and Etsuyo Michida[1]

2.1   INTRODUCTION

Across the world, governments and businesses have been developing policy initiatives to address environmental challenges, often under the general label of "sustainability." Many such initiatives have originated in Western countries, taking the form of multi-stakeholder coalitions that bring together business actors and non-governmental organizations (NGOs). These are often referred to as private regulation (Cafaggi and Janczuk, 2010), or civil regulation (Vogel, 2010), or "private standards,"[2] but the term "non-state market-driven" (NSMD) governance systems (Bernstein and Cashore, 2007; Cashore et al., 2007) more accurately describes their key features. They are created by non-state actors and rely on market forces to propagate the adoption of particular rules for how commodities should be grown, processed and traded. NSMD standards can be used to achieve a range of objectives, including food safety, product quality, animal welfare and sustainability (Henson and Humphrey, 2010).

Sustainability standards are designed to promote production practices that eliminate or mitigate possible negative impacts such as deforestation, loss of biodiversity, greenhouse gas emissions and damage to both communities and the environment more generally. By promoting consumer awareness about the risks of unsustainable production and shifting consumption choices towards products that adopt the standards, key businesses in commodity value chains—above all consumer-facing businesses whose brands are vulnerable to consumer and NGO pressure—then make such standards a precondition for access to their supply chains. This access requirement then puts pressure on businesses in commodity exporting countries to comply with the requirements set out by the standard and enforced by the standards scheme.[3] The mobilization of such consumer pressure is, however, uneven, with extensive consumer mobilization restricted to Western Europe and North America.

In the first decade of the 21st century one particular type of NSMD standard, Roundtable initiatives, brought together multiple stakeholders to develop sustainability standards for widely traded commodities. This chapter focuses on the most high-profile of these, the Roundtable on Sustainable Palm Oil (RSPO). This was created in 2004 by a multi-stakeholder coalition that brought together producers, processors, investors, retailers and NGOs. The RSPO developed the "Principles and Criteria for the Production of Sustainable Palm Oil," the first version of which was finalized and published in 2007 (Roundtable on Sustainable Palm Oil, 2007).

More recently, the model of private regulation used by Roundtable initiatives has been challenged by new standards developed by public actors in commodity exporting countries. In 2011, the Indonesian government launched the Indonesian Sustainable Palm Oil standard (ISPO), and in 2013 the Malaysian government created the Malaysian Sustainable Palm Oil standard (MSPO). The emergence of these two state-promoted standards developed by commodity exporting countries (alongside similar producer-developed initiatives, such as the Soja Plus standard created by Brazilian agribusiness associations) has generated a lot of discussion about what they are aiming to do and what their impact will be on NSMD standards and sustainability initiatives more generally.

In a discussion of the emergence of national standards for palm oil and soy, Hospes identifies two key questions:

> Do the new national sustainability standards in Indonesia and Brazil provide a fundamental challenge to the RSPO and the RTRS [Round Table on Responsible Soy], or do they demonstrate the successful diffusion and adoption of global private standards into national contexts? Do the new national sustainability standards help or undermine the RSPO and RTRS in their efforts to reduce de-forestation? (Hospes, 2014: 426)

This framing of the issue sets up a rivalry between national and NSMD standards. Hospes goes on to argue that "The government of Indonesia, as the world's largest producer and exporter of palm oil, is challenging the RSPO both nationally and internationally as the legitimate political authority to define and promote sustainable palm oil" (2014: 435), and also observes that "The underlying message [of national standards] is securing 'profit' first, then 'planet,' but not the other way around" (2014: 434). Similarly, Wijaya and Glasbergen (2016: 231) argue that "ISPO is certainly not part of a race to the top in promoting sustainability," and Bitzer and Schouten frame the issue as one of national standards acting as "challenger" or "rival" initiatives to established multi-stakeholder partnerships (2017: 3). Such views are supported by comparisons that highlight differences between the RSPO and the national standards, particularly with respect to planting in primary forests, protection of areas with high conservation values (Wijaya and Glasbergen, 2016: 232) and free, prior and informed consent (PFIC) (Hidayat et al., 2018; Hospes, 2014: 430).

Focusing on palm oil, this chapter frames the issue in a different way. It accepts that in the early stages of the development of national standards this process was partly motivated by concerns about the impact of the RSPO on producers and a desire to shift the balance between producer and consumer interests. However, it argues that national standards have evolved since their introduction, with rural development and poverty reduction issues becoming more central. This raises questions about the motivations behind the development of national standards, what is required for their implementation and how effective they might be.

The arguments in this chapter are based on an extensive review of the literature on palm oil standard schemes as well as interviews with respondents working in the palm oil sector based in a number of Asian countries—China, India, Indonesia, Malaysia and Japan. Respondents included government officials with responsibility for palm oil, palm oil industry bodies in both Indonesia and Malaysia, industry analysts, and standards organizations and NGOs in the region.

Section 2.2 discusses the motivations behind the creation of national standards, identifying both dissatisfactions with the operation of the RSPO and what the alternative standards might offer. Section 2.3 examines trends in palm oil exports from Indonesia and Malaysia and asks the question "How might national standards promote or obstruct access to different export markets?" Section 2.4 focuses on development goals and poverty alleviation, posing the question "Can national standards achieve the goal of incorporating smallholder farmers into certification schemes?" Section 2.5 considers the effectiveness of the national standards as schemes that could provide credible assurances about sustainable production and processing of palm oil. Section 2.6 concludes.

2.2   THE EMERGENCE OF NATIONAL SUSTAINABILITY STANDARDS FOR PALM OIL

Palm oil is used in food, animal feed, cosmetics, pharmaceuticals and for other industrial uses. In addition, it can be used as a biofuel or bioliquid. Malaysia and Indonesia are the world's largest exporters of palm oil, accounting for 90% of global exports in 2019.[4] Between 2000 and 2015 total palm oil production rose by 50% in Malaysia and almost 400% in Indonesia.[5] Palm oil is grown on large plantations, small plantations and on smallholder plots. Its production provides direct employment for many people, as well as generating downstream employment in processing, and it constitutes an important part of the rural economy in the two countries (Vis et al., 2012: 739–40). As well as generating significant export revenues, palm oil production has enabled diversification of the rural economy and has been a key element for poverty reduction and rural development.

At the same time, however, the rapid expansion of palm oil production has been linked to serious environmental problems, including deforestation, loss of biodiversity, threats to endangered animal species and increasing the greenhouse gas emissions that drive global heating, as well as negative impacts on local communities, workers and smallholders (Vis et al., 2012: 743–9). In the late 1990s extensive forest fires in Indonesia were linked by the World Wildlife Fund (WWF) to land clearances for palm oil production, with the acceptability of palm oil production and export being brought into question. However, subsequent interactions between the WWF, European companies using palm oil in their products and producers moved toward sustainable palm oil production and the supporting formation of the Roundtable on Sustainable Palm Oil in 2004. The RSPO's stakeholders included palm oil producers, processors and traders, consumer goods manufacturers, retailers, banks and investors and environmental/social NGOs.[6] By 2007 the RSPO had finalized its principles and criteria for sustainable palm oil production and a certification scheme to operationalize it (Roundtable on Sustainable Palm Oil, 2007).

The RSPO is an NSMD standard that aims to use the leverage of market access to drive the introduction of sustainable practices that are enforced by certification. As is common with such standards, the RSPO has evolved over time, with elements added to comply with the EU RED (Renewable Energy Directive, EU Directive 2009/28/EC) sustainability requirements for biofuels and bioliquids,[7] and the RSPO Next that introduces stricter controls over deforestation and emissions of greenhouse gases (Pacheco et al., 2020: 578).

The initial response of the governments of Indonesia and Malaysia to the development of the RSPO was not one of hostility. The Indonesian government's first reaction was to view private standards as a business matter that did not require government involvement, and from 2006 onwards there was collaboration between the RSPO and the Indonesian government to manage interactions and consider how the RSPO might best be implemented in the Indonesian context (Wijaya and Glasbergen, 2016: 227–30). However, five years later, in 2011, the ISPO was launched.

Part of the explanation for this shift revolves around disillusion in relation to the initial expectations of what the RSPO standard would offer to palm oil exporting countries. First, the exporting countries expected the RSPO to push back against campaigns that actively sought to limit or reduce palm oil production. The standard would legitimize palm oil production by providing assurances about sustainability. In fact, NGOs such as Greenpeace and Friends of the Earth (FOE) criticized both the RSPO and some of the companies most closely associated with it (such as Unilever) for setting requirements too low and for failing to provide effective enforcement. A press release issued by FOE in conjunction with the 2009 RSPO meeting in Malaysia referred to the RSPO scheme as being "full of loopholes" (Friends of the Earth International, 2009). In the face of such criticisms, producers became disillusioned:

> Producers who largely joined the [RSPO] initiative to combat negative publicity now see the leading certified companies becoming targets for further attacks. Rather than the shelter they expected, RSPO has begun to be perceived as a way to be singled out for not complying with specified criteria. (Nikoloyuk et al., 2010: 69)

This disillusion was further intensified by both the tightening up of both the RSPO's principles and criteria and its enforcement mechanisms—in large part as in response to clear evidence of continuing deforestation and land conflicts, above all in Indonesia (Teoh, 2010: 22). Governments, particularly in Europe, and NGOs such as WWF pressured for tighter standards and controls (Gnych et al., 2015: 8; Hutabarat et al., 2019: 256).

Second, the financial viability of the RSPO's certification scheme for palm oil producers and mills was based, in part, on the idea that the premium for certified sustainable palm oil (CSPO) would be sufficient to offset the costs of meeting the standard's requirements and of the certification process itself. This expectation was only partly fulfilled. Initially, demand for CSPO exceeded supply, with the premium ranging from $10 to $50 per ton across the three options for demonstrating sustainability (book and claim, mass balance and segregated) (WWF, 2012: 32). However, the supply of certified sustainable palm oil quickly outstripped market demand. As a result, the price premium dropped substantially—in the case of mass balance and segregated CSPO, by between 50% and 75% (WWF, 2012: 33). Excess supply also meant that producers could not find buyers for all of their CSPO, and by the end of 2011 only half of certified supply was sold into markets recognizing and paying for CSPO.[8] While the same WWF study points to additional and unanticipated benefits of RSPO certification, including increased operational efficiency, improved quality and reductions in pesticide use and accident rates among workers, these benefits were less tangible and more open to contention than the headline price premium. The study concluded that:

> The overstock of available CSPO in the market and the excess CSPO production capacity—with the resulting decline in premiums—have given growers cause for concern in their efforts to continue to certify under their RSPO time-bound plan commitments. (WWF, 2012: 33)

These issues led producers and governments in Malaysia and Indonesia to express dissatisfaction with the RSPO, and some of their critiques were couched in terms of the narrative of rivalry and replacement discussed above.

Public authorities argued that stakeholder representation in the RSPO favored downstream stakeholders in the value chain at the expense of those in the producing countries. When the Indonesian plantation companies association, GAPKI, withdrew from the RSPO following the creation of the ISPO, one of its justifications was that the RSPO standard was unable to accommodate producer interests (Giessen et al., 2016: 81). Similarly, GAPKI "criticised the RSPO for being too much in favour of green groups (i.e. pro-environmental NGOs and political parties)" (Kadarusman and Pramudya, 2019: 7), and this argument was also expressed in terms of the correct balance between people, profit and planet in the context of the legitimate development objectives of the two governments. Indonesian and Malaysian officials have repeatedly stressed that palm oil is an important crop for the country's economic development, with palm oil producers widely spread across both countries, including in areas with high levels of poverty. Therefore, sustainability standards in low-income countries should consider their impacts on poverty reduction and livelihoods, as well as focusing on environmental protection and climate change mitigation.[9]

The ISPO, launched in 2011 by The Ministry of Agriculture of Indonesia with support from the United Nations Development Programme (UNDP), is based on the application of national laws that are enforced by public agencies. Reflecting the concerns just outlined, the ISPO Commission defined its aims as "to improve the competitiveness of the Indonesian palm oil on the global market and contribute to the objectives set by the President of the Republic to reduce greenhouse gases emissions and draw attention to environmental issues" (quoted in Sahide et al., 2015: 163–4).

The national certification scheme for Malaysia, the MSPO, followed in 2013. It was set up as a standards scheme owned and managed by a newly created organization, The Malaysian Palm Oil Certification Council (MPOCC). The governing body of the MPOCC includes representatives from The Ministry of Plantation Industries and Commodities (MPIC), The Malaysian Palm Oil Board (MPOB), academia, R&D institutions, non-governmental organizations, oil palm industry associations, smallholder organizations and civil society. One observer characterized the MSPO and its relationship to the RSPO in the following terms:

> The [MSPO] initiative aims to differentiate Malaysian palm oil from that produced in other countries, while offering a less stringent alternative to the Roundtable on Sustainable Palm Oil ... The RSPO is more of a burden to the industry. It has certain conditions that are too stringent, it is very costly, and they keep changing their goals. The premium that we get is also minimum. (Butler, 2013: 1)

With such arguments being widely expressed, it is not surprising that much of the discussion about the new national palm oil standards has focused on the extent to which they undermine or weaken the commitment to sustainability and the approach of the RSPO (see, for example, Barthel et al., 2018; McInnes, 2017; Ministry of Agriculture of the Republic of Indonesia, 2015; Watts and Irawan, 2018).

However, a consideration of the characteristics of NSMD standards in general puts a different light on the challenges facing producer countries and how they might be addressed. The overall goals of the RSPO are to promote sustainable production and protect global forest resources. As an NSMD standard, it aims to achieve these goals by tapping into consumer and business concerns about sustainability. More specifically, it seeks to promote the adoption of sustainable sourcing practices by consumer-facing businesses in those countries (mostly higher income countries, particularly in Western Europe) where consumer awareness can be mobilized. Businesses make commitments to purchase palm oil certified to the RSPO standard. Making such commitments exposes these businesses to risks. If the standard is shown to be ineffective or poorly enforced then a high-profile brand could be accused of using unsustainably produced palm oil, lacking a genuine commitment to sustainability and deceiving its customers.[10] These are serious risks for businesses whose reputation for trustworthiness sustains their brand image and customer loyalty. Therefore, businesses minimize such risks by insisting on strict and enforceable standards, even if this raises cost and complexity for producers. At the same time, the priority for these businesses may be to establish the sustainability of the palm oil that they are purchasing, not to increase sustainability overall.

The international NGO, Solidaridad, and above all the Asian component of its international network, has characterized this approach to certification as "raising the bar" (Roozen, 2018). Access to export markets is made more demanding by the application of the standard. This creates two problems for producers and producing countries. First, the benefits of sustainability standards are confined to the production units that are supplying the market for certified sustainable palm oil. This limits the transformative potential of such standards. Second, compliance with NSMD standards is particularly problematic for smallholder producers who lack the capabilities and resources to meet the requirements set out by NSMD standards—both with respect to the resources needed to implement particular sustainability practices and the generation of documentation to show that the practices have been followed correctly and continuously. This has consequences for both rural development and sustainability, and, above all, for smallholder farmer livelihoods.

The smallholder farmer issue is pressing for both Indonesia and Malaysia. Smallholder farmers were responsible for approximately 40% of planted palm oil area in both countries in 2017.[11] In Malaysia, the area cultivated by independent smallholders almost doubled between 2003 and 2013 (Ador et al., 2016: 107), while in Indonesia smallholder farmers have contributed substantially to the overall expansion of palm oil production. It has also been argued in the case of Indonesia that "Among smallholders, the substantial increase in oil palm production was achieved mainly through the expansion of plantations on peatlands and into forest areas, because most of the mineral soils are cultivated by large-scale companies" (Hutabarat et al., 2018: 683). From the government perspective, broader social and development goals would be undermined if smallholders were marginalized from palm oil production. Equally, not addressing the smallholder farmer question would undermine the achievement of environmental goals as well. Can NSMD standards successfully incorporate smallholder farmers?

The difficulties of incorporating smallholder farmers into NSMD standards schemes have been widely documented. A systematic literature review on the impact of private (i.e. NSMD) standards on smallholder farmers commissioned by the International Trade Centre in Geneva examined 63 articles on the impact of private standards across a range of sectors, including coffee, flowers, fresh fruit and vegetables, and forestry products. On the issue of whether such standards tend to exclude small farmers. It concluded that:

> The majority of authors seem to agree that stringent quality and safety standards endanger small farmer participation in global value chains. This is because sourcing from a large number of small farmers is more difficult for companies, for several reasons: (i) higher transaction costs for monitoring conformity, (ii) need for more intensive farm extension, and (iii) need for financial resources. In general, vertical integration might benefit small producers by increasing income, productivity and product quality, providing guaranteed prices and sales, and improving access to capital. Nevertheless, evidence shows that these benefits are hypothetical as vertical integration in many cases led to the exclusion of small farmers. (von Hagen and Alvarez, 2011: 22–3)

Other studies (Ouma, 2010; Swinnen and Kuijpers, 2019) have reached similar conclusions, and the challenges lie in four main areas:

1. It is administratively and organizationally more costly and complex to incorporate numerous small farmers into certified supply chains than it is to use a much smaller number of large farms or plantations. Where large farm or plantations exist, they will generally have a cost advantage relative to small producers.
2. The costs and complexity increase further if there is a gap between existing small farmer capabilities and those required to implement standards requirements. Even if smallholder farmers are incorporated

into commodity supply chains, there is likely to be a bias in favor of small-holders that are better educated and have more resources.

3. Experience with standards implementation suggests that the viability of smallholder certification depends upon the development of collective organization through cooperatives, specialist produce marketing organizations (PMOs) or outgrower schemes managed by large farms (or plantations) or processing businesses (Humphrey, 2008). These are also difficult to develop and manage.

4. As was noted above, smallholder palm oil production has depended, in part, on expansion into peatlands and forest areas, which raises issues about land titles and sustainability.

In spite of attempts to incorporate smallholder farmers (Brandi et al., 2015) and measures taken to simplify certification procedures for these farmers (Pramudya et al., 2018: 6), rates of certification for smallholder farmers remain low relative to overall palm oil production and farmed area. Globally, RSPO claimed a total of 160,256 certified smallholders in 2020, with a land area totaling 452,933 ha.[12] This compares to a total certified land area of 4.3 million ha (ten times greater). Similarly, the number of RSPO-certified smallholders globally, 160,000, is low in comparison with the more than 2 million smallholder palm oil producers in Indonesia alone. The RSPO's data also highlight the importance of group formation to the success of certification schemes. Most of the smallholders holding RSPO certification across the world were organized into schemes, as can be seen in Table 2.1. In April 2020, independent smallholders accounted for just 5% of the total number of certified smallholder farms (with the rest being organized into schemes), 6.7% of the total area covered and 6% of smallholder output.[13]

Table 2.1   RSPO smallholder certification by type, April 2020

	Number of farms	Area (ha)	Output (metric tons)[a]
Scheme smallholders	152 070	372 435	6 701 001
Independent smallholders	8 186	26 650	427 464
Independent smallholder share (%)	5.1	6.7	6.0

Note: [a] Output in certified fresh fruit bunches.
Source: https://rspo.org/smallholders/smallholder-certification-in-numbers (last accessed May 2020).

The relevance of the challenges outlined above is shown by a study of four RSPO certification projects in Sumatra. This identified "five RSPO requirements that will be difficult to achieve for independent smallholders in view of current practices concerning land titles, seedlings, pesticide usage, fertiliza-tion, and documentation" (Brandi et al., 2015: 304). Land titles are a particu-larly complex issue in Indonesia because of lack of formalization of ownership and the spread of farming activities into prohibited areas,[14] but the other issues raised by Brandi et al. highlight the ways in which compliance with RSPO standards requires changes in production practices and documentation that would require substantial support from agricultural extension services for smallholder farmers, while also burdening smallholder farmers with increased costs that might not be offset by increased revenues. A case study of RSPO group certification in Indonesia for an association of three village cooperatives in 2012–13 showed that the benefits of certification (improved yields, higher prices) were offset by increased costs, resulting in lower net farm income following certification (Hutabarat et al., 2018).

In this context, Solidaridad has framed the challenge facing palm oil pro-ducing countries as one of simultaneously increasing smallholder participation and reducing environmental damage.[15] This is called "raising the floor." In contrast to "raising the bar," this policy is concerned with improving the efficiency and sustainability of smallholder production, extending markets for sustainable palm oil and enabling small farmers to gain access to these markets. This would combine environmental benefits with poverty reduction and moving to the achievement of the SDGs.

Two changes in the nature of national standards point to these consider-ations as drivers of their creation and modification. First, the ISPO scheme, which had been voluntary, was made mandatory for palm oil mills and plan-tations over 25 ha in Indonesia, with an initial cut-off date for certification set for 2014. Second, smallholders (under 25 ha) were included in the scope of mandatory certification, with the deadline for certification set for 2020 (Jong, 2018).[16] The MSPO followed suit: it became mandatory in 2017, with plans for a phased introduction to cover processing facilities, plantations and smallhold-ers by December 2019.

The combination of mandatory coverage and inclusion of smallholder farms would, if successfully implemented, extend sustainability certification to all producers and processors in the world's two largest palm oil exporting countries. This would provide a level of certification that NSMD standards have found impossible to achieve.[17] However, further examination is required about the feasibility of the strategies. Section 2.3 looks at global market trends for palm oil. If global markets are shifting away from areas of strength of the RSPO, does this open up opportunities for national standards? Section 2.4 examines the viability of national standards, and in particular the challenges of extending certification to smallholder farmers. Section 2.5 considers the ques-tion of standards implementation and the obstacles to creating credible and enforceable standards. These three sections then make it possible to return to the question of the motivations behind the development of national standards.

2.3   NATIONAL PALM OIL STANDARDS AND MARKET ACCESS

The effectiveness of NSMD standards depends upon market acceptance, and the RSPO has been very successful in the European market. CSPO is widely demanded by food processors and retailers: 69% of palm oil imported for food consumption in Europe was certified sustainable in 2016.[18] The tendency is for this position to strengthen. Commitments already made through the European Palm Oil Alliance and the Amsterdam Declaration (2015) should raise certification to 100% by 2020 (Roundtable on Sustainable Palm Oil, 2018: 67). Although there are a number of certification schemes for palm oil, European Union (EU) countries generally equate palm oil sustainability with RSPO certification. For example, UK government guidance on palm oil posed the question "What is sustainable palm oil?" answering with the statement "In practice, the market for sustainable palm oil is dominated by the Roundtable for Sustainable Palm Oil (RSPO), and so the term is commonly understood to mean products certified to RSPO standards and criteria" (Department for Environment Food and Rural Affairs, 2017: 2).

RSPO certification reaches beyond Europe. In the case of Japan, for example, one leading retailer has already moved to using RSPO-certified palm oil, and other large retailers committed to do so in 2020.[19] There is also a substantial global market for biomass that could be supplied from the residues of palm oil production (particularly palm oil kernels) (Junginger et al., 2020), and in the case of Japan, the biomass sustainability program had accepted RSPO certification as demonstrating sustainability for the purposes of Feed-in-Tariff policy by 2018. In 2020 it had still not recognized either the ISPO or MSPO, although a reconsideration of their status after 2021 was left open by the Japanese authorities. Furthermore, the RSPO is used by investment funds as an indicator of responsible and sustainable investment. Given that the investment requirements of palm oil businesses in Malaysia and Indonesia exceed the funding capacity of the local market, there is pressure on larger local businesses to use RSPO certification as the legitimate indicator of sustainability.[20] Not surprisingly, many palm oil businesses (growers, processors, etc.) in both Malaysia and Indonesia remained RSPO certified even after certification to the national standards became mandatory, with more than 3 million ha of production across the two countries certified in 2019.[21] This is accepted by national authorities. The Malaysian Palm Oil Certification Council has, for example, produced a guidance document on combined audits for MSPO and RSPO certification (MPOCC, 2018).

Access to the markets of developed countries is a key driver for the adoption of NSMD standards. As was argued in Chapter 1 of this volume, the most straightforward way of achieving market access is for exporting businesses to adopt the standards required by their customers. Failing this, such businesses should adopt equivalent (and benchmarked) standards as a means of securing access. If countries develop similar but not identical standards through the processes of learning and emulation, market access is undermined, and the introduction of modified standards is associated with attending to domestic priorities and the capabilities of local businesses.

The ISPO and MSPO standards do differ from the RSPO in certain important respects, but the palm oil industries in both countries are highly export oriented. What, then, is the logic of developing local standards, and are they likely to secure access to export markets? The continuing dominance of the RSPO in Europe indicates that the chances of supplanting it as the acceptable benchmark for sustainability would, at the very least, require some convergence of the two national standards towards the principles and criteria of the RSPO. Without this, the standards are best considered as relevant either to other destination markets and/or to domestic agendas. This section considers the potential role of national standards in facilitating exports to alternative destinations.

Markets outside of Europe and North America were identified as important for the RSPO from early on in its existence. In the year that the principles and criteria were finalized, 2007, EU imports of crude palm oil (CPO) totaled just under 5 million metric tons, but imports into India and China totaled 9.6 million metric tons.[22] By 2019, the respective figures were 7000 and 16,950 tons, when the 27 countries of the EU accounted for only 14.2% of global CPO imports. In 2011, a presentation at Roundtable 9 (RT9) highlighted the need to extend certification to developing economies if the RSPO was going to achieve its vision "To transform the market for palm oil so that Certified Sustainable Palm Oil becomes the norm" (Teoh, 2011). The following year, Vis et al. (2012: 778) cited work from Oxfam International suggesting that raising global demand for certified palm oil to 40% of all consumption by 2019 would require China to use certified oil for 40% of its consumption. More recently, Kadarusman and Pramudya (2019: 903) put RSPO objectives for CSPO consumption in China and India at 10% and 30% respectively.

These targets have not been reached. The RSPO's own data show that sales of CSPO by RSPO members in both China and India were extremely low, as shown in Table 2.2. RSPO members were responsible for 8% and 28% of total palm oil imports into China and India respectively (line D of the table), but most of this was non-certified. This is particularly the case in India, where less than 1% of RSPO members' own imports were certified. As a result, the share of RSPO-certified palm oil in total palm oil imports was 1.1% in China

Table 2.2   *RSPO members' palm oil (HS 1511) imports into China and India in 2017*

	China (000 tons)	India (000 tons)
A. Total imports from Malaysia and Indonesia	5077	8979
B. RSPO member total imports	420	2512
C. RSPO member imports of RSPO-certified oil	56.3	7.9
D. RSPO members share of total imports (= (B)/(A)*100)	8.3%	27.98%
E. RSPO-certified share of RSPO member imports (= (C)/(B)*100)	13.4%	0.3%
F. RSPO member imports of RSPO-certified oil /total palm oil imports (=(C)/(A)*100)	1.1%	0.09%

Source: Authors, created from the RSPO homepage and UN COMTRADE.

and 0.09% in India (line F).[23] The global impact of this is that the share of RSPO-certified palm oil in global palm oil sales remains under 20%, in spite of earlier targets to raise this to 40%.[24]

The reasons for the absence of a substantial market for certified palm oil in both China and India have been discussed at length by Schleifer and Sun (2018) and Kadarusman and Pramudya (2019). Schleifer and Sun argue that the likelihood of the emergence of effective NSMD standards depends on a combination of market and non-market conditions (2018: 193–6). The market conditions are consumer perceptions in the destination market and the characteristics of business actors along the value chain, including the incidence of concentration and branding in the destination market, concentration among traders and the role of peak industry associations. The non-market conditions are social movement pressure, the capacity of public and private governance institutions and the role of foreign governments and intergovernmental organizations. These factors have facilitated the development of standards in Western Europe but constrain their development in both India and China. In India, in particular, Schleifer and Sun (2018: 204–5) point to price-sensitive consumers,[25] a fragmented distribution system, low levels of commitment to sustainability on the part of big food businesses and lack of support from the peak industry association in the edible oils sector, the Solvent Extractors Association of India. The same authors also point to non-market factors that further restrict the penetration of RSPO.

The inability of RSPO-certified palm oil to gain penetration in the Chinese and Indian markets might appear to offer an opening for the ISPO and MSPO, but they may face the same challenges. Is there potential for promoting national sustainability certifications in these markets when the RSPO certification has so signally failed? One argument, advanced by Kadarusman and Pramudya, is that China and India are still at a stage where consumption of scarce natural resources is seen as necessary for economic growth, but that at some higher level of socio-economic values this will change and consumers and policymakers will make stronger commitments to sustainability (2019: 8). In other words, rising incomes and welfare will be sufficient to change private and public attitudes to sustainability and increase the willingness to pay for sustainable products.

Public authorities in both Indonesia and Malaysia act as if it is possible, even now, to develop markets for CSPO in China and India. The strategy focuses on businesses rather than consumers. The Palm Oil Boards of both Indonesia and Malaysia signed Memoranda of Understanding (MOU) with the Solvent Extractors Association of India and the international NGO Solidaridad in 2018 and 2019. The MOU with Indonesia recognizes the ISPO and the Indian Palm Oil Sustainability (IPOS) Framework as being "legitimate sustainability frameworks for palm oil production and trade between Indonesia and India" (Solidaridad, 2018), while the MOU with Malaysia defines its objective as jointly promoting the two standards (MSPO and IPOS) through a process of harmonization.[26] Similarly, a Malaysian media source has referred to a government-negotiated barter deal between China and Malaysia. This would promote palm oil exports and recognize MSPO-certified palm oil products as qualified to use the Chinese "green food" label.[27] However, some six to eight years after the development of the two national standards, these agreements are still at the MOU stage, and formal agreements have yet to be reached.

If the narrative of rivalry and replacement is correct and the motivation behind the development of both standards was to rival the RSPO in destination markets, then that objective has failed in Europe and North America and has yet to achieve significant gains in China and India. Furthermore, the dynamics of these markets have contrasting implications for the further development of the standards. Levelling up is required for Europe in order to match the credibility of the RSPO, while it seems clear that little or no premium can be expected in China or in India. The trade case for national standards appears to be weak. The influence of domestic considerations on their development needs to be explored.

2.4 NATIONAL STANDARDS AND SMALLHOLDER CERTIFICATION

The extension of certification to all smallholder farmers in both Indonesia and Malaysia has two goals: increasing the sustainability of national palm oil production by extending controls to a much broader category of producers, and raising the productivity and efficiency of smallholder palm oil producers so as to improve livelihoods and promote rural transformation. However, Section 2.2 highlighted both the difficulties in incorporating smallholder farmers into a range of different standard schemes and the limited success encountered by the RSPO with respect to smallholder inclusion. The broader literature on certification identifies challenges relating to cost, the levels of knowledge required to implement standards at the farm level, the broader issues of capability, market structure and smallholder organization. In the case of palm oil, land titles and land use are further issues.

In both Indonesia and Malaysia, financial support is seen as essential for improving smallholder farmer performance and compliance, and both countries' programs support not only certification, but other performance improvements. In July 2019 the Indonesian government "agreed to bear the costs incurred by smallholder farmers for obtaining Indonesia Sustainable Palm Oil (ISPO) certification" and that this funding would "help smallholders obtain certification and ensure good agricultural practices" (Aisyah, 2019). Similarly, the Malaysian Palm Oil Board (MPOB) "provides financial assistance including full coverage of certification cost, cost of Personal Protective Equipment (PPE) and chemical store/rack," as well as technical assistance (Senawi et al., 2019: 501). In other words, certification and improvements in production practices require technical assistance.

The challenges do not stop here, particularly for independent farmers. While some have the capabilities and resources required, many do not. Detailed studies of independent smallholder preparedness for certification among farmers in Kalimantan in Indonesia show that while a substantial minority (43%) have the resources and experience to meet the requirements of the ISPO and take advantage of the state and private sector support on offer, for an equally significant number of farmers (38%) "The cost and complexity of ISPO compliance will for many be prohibitive and replanting financially and arguably socially undesirable" (Schoneveld et al., 2019: 15). This is not solely an issue of education or experience, but has deeper structural roots, as highlighted by Jelsma et al.:

> The second major upgrading challenge relates to the mechanisms through which smallholders access credit, production inputs, and knowledge. Though not comprehensively assessed in this article, the low yields, use of poor quality planting

material and variable inputs, and failure to adopt best management practices across all groups of the typology certainly undermines smallholder productivity, profitability, and environmental performance potential. (Jelsma et al., 2017: 293)

Further, land titles have been particularly problematic in Indonesia (for a recent discussion of this issue, see Jong, 2020). Although establishing the legality of land ownership is a requirement of the ISPO, many smallholder farmers do not possess the correct documentation, and a proportion of increased production in recent years has taken place through illegal land occupation. Recent surveys of smallholders in Riau Province have shown that 54% of surveyed smallholders were not compliant with land documentation requirements (Jelsma et al., 2017: 292), while in Kalimantan 61% of smallholders did not possess nationally recognized land documentation (Schoneveld et al., 2019: 12).

In both countries, the formation of organized smallholder farmer groups is a central pillar of strategies for improving the livelihoods and efficiency of smallholder farmers. The development of such groups predates the development of national standards and their later extension to smallholder farmers. In Malaysia, smallholder palm oil producers are defined as operating plantations of under 100 acres (approximately 40 ha) and having a land title or operating under customary rights (Rosniza Aznie et al., 2018: 70). Approximately 60% of these smallholders are those incorporated into a variety of resettlement and rehabilitation programs that are linked to specific palm oil mills that provide support to their farmer groups (Kailany, 2011). In Indonesia, a Ministry of Agriculture regulation defines smallholders as working an area under 25 ha, although most smallholders have plots of less than 4 ha (Hutabarat, 2017). Organized smallholders have been incorporated into a number of different programs, public and private, to link small farmers to larger estates:

> These programs typically included the establishment of a so-called nucleus estate, that is, a large-scale plantation with a central oil palm processing facility or mill, and surrounding scheme smallholders from which oil palm was sourced and for whom the nucleus provided and prepared the land, planted seedlings, and carried out maintenance until the trees started to produce fruits. Scheme smallholders have to manage the plantation under the nucleus' supervision and must sell their oil palm fruits to the nucleus' mill. (Hutabarat et al., 2019: 254)

These organized smallholders are often referred to as plasma producers, which derives from the nucleus estates model developed in the 1980s (Jelsma et al., 2017: 282).

Certification levels are substantially higher for organized smallholders. In August 2019, MSPO certification rates had reached 56% for organized smallholders, but only 6% for independent smallholders.[28] Similarly, the overwhelming majority of smallholders certified to the ISPO standard by 2015 were plasma smallholders (a total of 80,000), compared to just 3500 certified independent farmers (Stockholm Environment Institute, 2019). The extension of certification to all smallholder farmers is closely linked to the further extension of organized smallholder programs because it not only makes certification and the delivery of financial and technical support easier to provide, but also creates mechanisms for monitoring and control of smallholder performance and compliance.

In Malaysia, the MPOB began to promote farmer groups for palm oil, known as Sustainable Palm Oil Clusters (SPOCs) as early as 2009—prior to the development of the MSPO—but SPOCs were later adopted as the way forward to achieving MSPO group certification (Rahman, 2016). The arrangement also includes group management and control provided by the Quality Management Systems (QMSs) that are required for MSPO group certification.[29] In 2018 a Senior Research Fellow at the MPOB presented plans for all 250,000 independent smallholders to be grouped into 162 SPOCs, each consisting of between 1500 and 2000 smallholders (Kuntom, 2018). These SPOCs would be promoted and managed by a variety of organizations, including NGOs, industry actors and government, which would provide management, training, documentation, audit and corrective actions.

As has been the case with other initiatives for smallholder organization, there have been delays. By 2018 MSPO certification had been achieved for 60 SPOCs—half of the planned level of 120 for that year. Six weeks before the deadline of 2019 for achieving the final total of 162 SPOCs the *Borneo Post* was reporting that in Sarawak only 37% of smallholder farmers were in certified SPOCs, and that only 55% of all the independent smallholders in the State had been certified.[30] Such a wholesale transformation of the working relationships and capabilities of hundreds of thousands of smallholder farmers across the whole country presents substantial challenges.

These challenges are even larger in Indonesia, where there are up to 2 million independent smallholders, and the number of ISPO-certified smallholder groups was only six at the end of 2018 (Hidayat, 2018). In Indonesia the challenge is not only to work with so many farmers, but also to find enough organizations that are able and willing to provide the framework within which such a large social transformation can be achieved and successfully managed. It remains to be seen whether the authorities in Indonesia have the financial resources to subsidize certification and support the necessary investments by smallholder farmers, or the capabilities to enhance the skills of farmers so that they can both manage production and obtain the increased yields needed to make certification financially attractive.

Both countries are receiving support from outside bodies. The Solidaridad NGO signed an MOU with the MSPO in 2016 to promote sustainable production among smallholder producers,[31] and by 2020 Solidaridad, and the Dutch government's sustainable trade initiative IDH, had developed its NI-SCOPS program to work with smallholder palm oil producers and government agencies to achieve sustainability in Indonesia, Malaysia, Ghana and Nigeria (IDH and Solidaridad, 2020). It is too early to say how successful these programs will be, and conclusions about the benefits to smallholders of national certification and their sustainability impacts cannot be made until more evidence is available on implementation.

2.5   EFFECTIVE IMPLEMENTATION

While the discussion of the differences between the RSPO, ISPO and MSPO has often focused on standards design and what the standards are meant to achieve, a critical issue for any standards scheme is how effectively it is operationalized in the field. This leads to the third question, "Are the two national standards designed in such a way as to provide assurances that they will work effectively?"

Standards create behavioral rules that, if followed correctly, will produce a set of outcomes that achieve the multiple goals of the standard—for example, protection of peatlands, good environmental management and protection of livelihoods, particularly for the poor. A standard is a written document that provides "rules, guidelines or characteristics for activities or their result."[32] In order to be effective, a standard has to be administered and enforced—turned into a standards scheme. Dingwerth and Pattberg (2009: 711) argue that this requires four elements:

- Clear guidelines to identify obligations and conformance. The behavioral rules need to be "sufficiently precise to allow for a distinction between compliant and non-compliant behavior."
- Effective implementation of procedures for assessing compliance with the behavioral rules specified in the principles and criteria. Conformity assessment is usually conducted through audits of documentation and behavior.
- Management of non-conformance through transparent enforcement procedures that require corrective actions and/or sanctions.
- The organizations tasked with managing the standard possess the resources and capabilities necessary to carry out their responsibilities.

The creators of the MSPO adopted a strategy of following the certification rules set out by the ISO. The MS 2530-2013 set of standards is administered by a specialist agency set up for the task, managed by the MPOCC. It emphasizes its alignment with ISO 17021 on conformity assessment and ISO/IEC 17011 on the accreditation of certification bodies. The MSPO family of standards is reviewed once every five years, in line with the process of periodic reviews undertaken by NSMD standards (Kuntom, 2016). A review was scheduled for 2019–20, with the final draft and approval of changes scheduled for December 2020 (MPOCC, 2019). This provides an opportunity to review the MSPO's successes and failures and also consider how it might be aligned with the needs of different markets. Public bodies in Malaysia may look for ways to make the standard more robust, partly in order to gain wider international acceptance, and partly because of the increasing recognition of the importance of environmental management. If operated correctly, it should provide assurances about implementation equivalent to those provided by NSMD schemes.

The ISPO has taken a different route, and this raises questions about its implementation. Although claiming to follow internationally accepted principles for the management of certification schemes (Hidayat, 2018),[33] the ISPO was created around extensive, existing governmental regulations relating to palm oil in Indonesia that were developed from the 1970s onwards. Its mandatory nature means that the government can impose sanctions in case of non-compliance, which might be a stronger enforcement mechanism than that available to the RSPO (withdrawal of certification), but there are also weaknesses in implementation and oversight. In addition to the ambiguities created by the organization of a large, complex and evolving set of regulations into a standard, this approach distributes the responsibilities for monitoring and implication across a number of different national agencies and across multiple levels of government in a country that has gone further than most in decentralizing government activities. This results in a fragmentation of enforcement mechanisms, not only across different levels of government, but also between different ministries: the scheme's behavioral rules and enforcement mechanisms are "an accumulation of (national) rules under various ministries" (Hidayat et al., 2018: 228).

A detailed analysis of the governance and management of the ISPO by Hidayat et al. (2018) indicates a number of areas where the standard and its implementation scheme has failed to meet the requirements set out at the beginning of this section. First, do the guidelines provide the clarity required to distinguish between compliant and non-compliant behavior on a consistent basis? This is usually achieved by formulating critical control points in ways that allow clear yes/no responses to be given. Hidayat et al. argue that there are areas where the ISPO lacks clarity. For example:

> some of the ISPO's action points are still rather vague. An example can be found in the rule about biodiversity conservation where ISPO touches on the need for conservation management. However, neither the concept of conservation management, nor the corresponding managing practices, or the intensity of these activities are explicated. Related to this vagueness is the absence of clear and detailed technical instructions, which leads to different interpretations of the PnC [Principles and Criteria] by different auditors. (Hidayat et al., 2018: 227)

Second, are enforcement mechanisms adequate? While it may make sense to build on existing legislation, this has had the effect of distributing enforcement responsibilities across various ministries, undermining the ISPO, slowing down the enforcement process and making it subject to inter-institutional negotiation, conflicts of interest and bureaucratic pressures. Equally, it creates uncertainty about the distribution of responsibilities between the ISPO and multiple ministries. Third, the main sanctions applicable to a plantation's non-conformance with the ISPO's rules are the lowering of a plantation's grade or a withdrawal of the plantation's permit.[34] However, the authority to enforce sanctions in this area is a responsibility of local government (Hidayat et al., 2018: 229), and these authors point to both the limited availability of certification bodies and the fact that the obligations allocated to local government are not matched by the resources made available for fulfilling them. In particular, local government institutions do not have the information required to take a proactive role in identifying non-compliance.

Taken together, these observations cast doubt on the effectiveness of implementation. The last point about oversight is critical. NSMD standards work on the basis of a "presumption of guilt" (Humphrey, 2017: 30–1). It is up to the certified operation to provide proof that it complies with the behavioral rules set out by the standard. This compliance is checked regularly by inspections. Legal frameworks often work on the basis of a "presumption of innocence." It may, for example, be illegal under EU law for food business operators to import food into the EU that contains pesticide residues above legal limits. However, border inspections are limited, and action is unlikely to be taken until there is clear evidence of law-breaking. If local enforcement bodies lack the information and resources required to take a proactive role in monitoring producer behavior, as well as acting, in effect, on the basis of the presumption of innocence, then the degree of confidence that producers are complying with the regulations will be lower. The ability to conduct such enforcement activities may also be weakened if local administrations are subject to political influence. This issue has been discussed for the case of Indonesia in relation to forestry controls in general, and also with respect to landownership and documentation (Jelsma et al., 2017). Although these discussions are mainly concerned with the power of large businesses to suborn local governments, it does point to the more general weaknesses in enforcement capacity.

2.6   CONCLUSIONS

Chapter 1 examined the issue of policy diffusion and the spread of environmental and food safety standards. It highlighted the considerable spread of public regulations across jurisdictions and the different motivations that would lead to their adoption outside the countries where they were initially developed. The literature in this field identifies four different motivations for the adoption of public regulations by follower countries and by businesses. These lie on the continuum from voluntary adoption through processes of learning and emulation through to adoption driven by conditions in export markets—the competitiveness and coercion motivations. While the literature on policy diffusion has mostly focused on public policy, Chapter 1 highlighted the relevance of this discussion to private regulation, or NSMD standards.

As was noted in Chapter 1, the literature suggests that where market access is the main factor in policy diffusion (the competitiveness and coercion motivations), the process of diffusion is most likely to take the form of adopting the standards required in key export markets wholesale—either through compliance with external certification or through the development of equivalent and benchmarked local standards. In contrast, in cases where standards are adopted because of learning (understanding the benefits of standards and how they are developed) or emulation (adopting practices because of the legitimacy of earlier developers or adopters) there is more scope for adapting these standards to meet local priorities and local capabilities.

The development of national palm oil standards by the governments of Indonesia and Malaysia presents a challenge to this framework. These countries are the major exporters of palm oil, and as sustainability concerns grew in importance in destination markets, both countries were worried that acceptance among consumers, businesses and governments would decline, particularly in Europe. After initially supporting the development of the RSPO, both countries developed alternative standards. Given that these new standards were developed for a product largely destined for export markets, why did they not closely replicate the RSPO?

The analysis of trade in palm oil shows that supply and demand factors both played a role. NSMD standards are most effective where there are many suppliers competing for market share and where the requirements set out by particular destination markets have a big impact on the benefits available to exporting countries. The global market for palm oil is not like this. First, Section 2.3 showed that Indonesia and Malaysia supply approximately 85% of global palm oil exports. This could, in theory, reduce the options available to importing countries, although there are other vegetable oils available and there has been some increase in palm oil production in other countries. However, this concentration of supply and the development of national standards has neither undermined the EU's acceptance of the RSPO as a credible indicator of sustainable palm oil production nor led to recognition of the ISPO and MSPO as being equivalent to it. Access to the European market still depends on RSPO certification. Second, the standards requirements across global markets for palm oil are heterogeneous. Asian countries, particularly China and India, were more important markets for palm oil exports than Europe even prior to the formation of the RSPO (2004) and the finalization of its principles and conditions (2007). However, given the very limited market for CSPO in these countries, they have so far provided a very limited market for any type of certified palm oil, including palm oil with ISPO or MSPO certification. These markets are also unlikely to offer a price premium even if certification gains broader penetration in them.

If the initial goal of the two national standards was to undermine the RSPO and develop new standards that would be more acceptable to producers and/or be more appealing to consumers and businesses in the fast-growing markets of Asia, then the initiatives have not yet succeeded. Nevertheless, the national standards are being promoted as having an important role to play in the pursuit of sustainable rural development. Sustainable production of palm oil is a domestic concern for both Indonesia and Malaysia, and sustainability is linked to rural livelihoods and economic growth. Ideally, the strategy of smallholder farmer inclusion will change the trade-offs between sustainability, livelihoods and economic growth. The national standards substitute for the RSPO in terms of their intervention in the domestic sphere, where the RSPO's potential for rural transformation has been limited by its voluntary nature and the market mechanism itself, which restricts its effects to production for markets that require CSPO. While the RSPO has been very significant in developing the sustainability agenda for palm oil and has had an effect on attitudes and policies in both exporting and importing countries, it has been unable to promote demand for CSPO outside of high-income countries and unable to provide a certification system that would incorporate the majority of smallholder farmers.

The ISPO and MSPO have now positioned themselves as providing, or at least intending to provide, a solution to this challenge by combining national standards with mandatory coverage extended to all producers, including small-holder farmers. This, it is hoped, will increase overall sustainability of palm oil production while at the same time improving the livelihoods of the rural poor and increasing the efficiency of palm oil production. At present, this is work in progress. Mandatory certification for smallholder palm oil producers is still a goal whose implementation is planned for the next few years, but even when this is enacted into law there is no guarantee that the capabilities and commit-ment needed to implement and enforce it will be achieved at the farm level. The literature shows quite clearly that there are considerable gaps between the existing capabilities and resources of smallholder palm oil producers and what would be required to comply with the national standards. The challenge is to provide the technical support, financial assistance and group organization to smallholder farmers that would turn the stated goal to an achievable outcome. Success cannot be ruled out, but it is too early to know if this strategy will succeed in either Indonesia or Malaysia.

Finally, the implementation question is not solely about resources, but also about the effective management of the two standard schemes. Concerns about implementation have been raised, particularly with respect to Indonesia. It follows that it is too early to assess the effectiveness of the two schemes. Further, to the extent that there is continuing divergences between the requirements of European markets and the emerging and developing markets of Asia, any revisions to the national standard schemes will have to navigate the different requirements of these markets and consider how to balance the need for credible and rigorous sustainability principles and criteria with manageable costs and accessibility for smallholder farmers.

NOTES

1. The authors wish to thank key informants in Asia for providing extensive information about the palm oil sector. In particular, they would like to thank respondents from the Malaysian Palm Oil Board for their insightful observations, and Shatadru Chattopadhayay, Managing Director of Solidaridad Asia and Teoh Cheng Hai, Senior Adviser, Solidaridad Asia, and the Founding Secretary General of RSPO for the interviews they gave and for their detailed comments on an earlier version of this chapter. The authors alone are responsible for any remaining shortcomings.
2. The term "private standards" has been adopted extensively not only by researchers, but also by international organizations (Dankers, 2007; ISO, 2010; OECD, 2006; von Hagen and Alvarez, 2011; WTO, 2007).
3. The International Organisation for Standardisation (ISO) defines standards as "documented agreements containing technical specifications or other precise criteria to be used consistently as rules, guidelines or definitions, to ensure that materials, products, processes and services are fit for their purpose" (http://www.fao.org/docrep/006/y5136e/y5136e07.htm). A standards scheme makes a standard operational by devising rules and procedures for implementation, conformity assessment and enforcement.
4. Source: https://www.indexmundi.com/agriculture/?commodity=palm-oil&graph=exports&display=map.
5. IndexMundi.
6. According to one informant, the involvement of states was considered but excluded because of the expectation that this would be complex and time-consuming, rather than as a result of principled opposition to government involvement.
7. See https://rspo.org/certification/rspo-red.
8. While there have been fluctuations in supply and demand of certified palm oil, in 2018 the RSPO was asking its members to increase purchases of certified palm oil in order to avoid a likely excess of certified produce on the market (https://www.foodnavigator-asia.com/Article/2019/11/18/Supply-vs-demand-MNCs-urged-to-play-larger-role-in-easing-Asia-s-sustainable-palm-oil-oversupply).
9. A further development of this argument is to link sustainability initiatives to the United Nations Sustainable Development Goals (SDGs) (see, for example, Hidayat, 2018).
10. In 1997, a BBC program about child labor on farms in Zimbabwe supplying the British supermarket, Tesco, had a substantial impact in the UK (Hughes, 2001:

426). Even five years after the event, managers at fruit and vegetable suppliers in the UK interviewed by one of the authors frequently referred to this episode (unprompted by the interviewer) as the kind of incident that could lead to exclusion from supermarket supply chains and lasting damage to their businesses.

11. The figure for Indonesia, taken from Kadarusman and Pramudya (2019: 5), combines so-called "plasma producer," linked to large estates, and independent smallholders. For Malaysia, the 40% area (Rahman, 2016: 6) is split between 23% operated by organized smallholders and 17% for independent smallholders. Source: http://bepi.mpob.gov.my/images/area/2017/Area_summary.pdf.

12. All of the data in this paragraph are taken from https://rspo.org/smallholders.

13. The distinction between independent and scheme smallholders is discussed further below.

14. Some of the complex issues involved in showing legal ownership of land in Riau Province in Indonesia are discussed by Jelsma et al. (2017: 292).

15. See https://www.solidaridadnetwork.org/supply-chains/palm-oil.

16. This deadline was later delayed until 2025 (Jong, 2020).

17. In the case of Malaysia, for example, RSPO certifies approximately 1 million ha of production, while a mandatory MSPO standard could, in principle, reach a total area of almost 6 million ha.

18. https://www.idhsustainabletrade.com/news/europe-way-achieving-100-sustainable-palm-oil/

19. Information from interviews at a leading Japanese retailer and the Japan office of an international certification body providing RSPO traceability certification for operations in Japan.

20. This information comes from interviews with investment analysts based in Singapore and Malaysia.

21. https://rspo.org/impact.

22. Unless otherwise specified, the data in this section are taken from index mundi and referring to imports and exports of crude palm oil.

23. The RSPO's own calculations for 2018 put the share of RSPO-certified palm oil in total imports in China and India at 1.5% and 1% respectively.

24. https://rspo.org/impact

25. An interview conducted with an industry association for vegetable oil for food in Japan (September 11, 2019) indicated that depending on certification types, RSPO-certified oil price could be 30% higher than conventional oil.

26. Economic Times, September 27, 2019, https://economictimes.indiatimes.com/news/economy/agriculture/malaysian-and-indian-palm-oil-industry-join-hands-to-promote-sustainable-palm-oil-production-and-trade/articleshow/71334075.cms.

27. https://www.thestar.com.my/news/nation/2019/06/01/msia-strikes-palm-oil-barter-trade-deal-with-china/

28. Source: https://www.mpocc.org.my/mspo-certification.

29. This approach to group organization is quite common. For example, the GlobalG.A.P. standard has a long-standing QMS system for group certification (GLOBALG.A.P., 2019).

30. https://www.theborneopost.com/2019/11/14/oil-palm-smallholders-urged-to-apply-for-mspo-cert/.

31. https://www.solidaridadnetwork.org/news/solidaridad-joins-hands-with-malaysian-palm-oil-board-to-promote-sustainability.

32. https://www.iso.org/sites/ConsumersStandards/1_standards.html.

33. The author of the presentation, made at the 14th Indonesian Palm Oil Conference, Aziz Hidayat, was the chairman of the Secretariat of the ISPO Commission.
34. Concise descriptions of the ISPO certification process can be found in Hidayat et al. (2018: 236) and Harsono et al. (2012: 43–4).

REFERENCES

Ador, S.F., Siwar, C. and Ghazali, R. (2016). A review of palm oil impact on sustainability dimension: SPOC initiative for independent smallholders. *International Journal of Agriculture, Forestry and Plantation* 2, 104–10.

Aisyah, R. 2019, July 31. Govt to fully finance ISPO certification for smallholders. *Jakarta Post*. Retrieved from https://www.thejakartapost.com/news/2019/07/31/govt-to-fully-finance-ispo-certification-for-smallholders.html (last accessed June 2020).

Amsterdam Declaration (2015). Towards eliminating deforestation from agricultural commodity chains with European countries. Amsterdam. Retrieved from https://www.euandgvc.nl/documents/publications/2015/december/7/declarations (last accessed June 2020).

Barthel, M., Fry, J., Jennings, S. et al. (2018). Study on the environmental impact of palm oil consumption and on existing sustainability standards. Luxembourg: Publications Office of the European Union. Retrieved from https://publications.europa.eu/en/publication-detail/-/publication/89c7f3d8-2bf3-11e8-b5fe-01aa75ed71a1 (last accessed October 2019).

Bernstein, S. and Cashore, B. (2007). Can non-state global governance be legitimate? An analytical framework. *Regulation & Governance* 1(4), 347–71, doi: 10.1111/j.1748-5991.2007.00021.x.

Bitzer, V. and Schouten, G. (2017). Out of balance: Tensions in global multi-stakeholder partnerships and the formation of local competing organisations in emerging economies. Paper submitted to Workshop on Rising Powers and Labour Standards in Global Production Networks, Manchester, June 19–20.

Brandi, C., Cabani, T., Hosang, C., Schirmbeck, S., Westermann, L. and Wiese, H. (2015). Sustainability standards for palm oil: Challenges for smallholder certification under the RSPO. *Journal of Environment & Development* 24(3), 292–314, doi: 10.1177/1070496515593775.

Butler, R. (2013). Malaysia to launch palm oil certification scheme to compete with RSPO. Retrieved from https://news.mongabay.com/2013/09/malaysia-to-launch-palm-oil-certification-scheme-to-compete-with-rspo/ (last accessed October 2019).

Cafaggi, F. and Janczuk, A. (2010). Private regulation and legal integration: The European example. *Business and Politics* 12(3), article 6.

Cashore, B., Auld, G., Bernstein, S. and McDermott, C. (2007). Can non-state governance "ratchet up" global environmental standards? Lessons from the forest sector. *Review of European Comparative & International Environmental Law* 16(2), 158–72, doi: 10.1111/j.1467-9388.2007.00560.x.

Dankers, C. (2007). Private standards in the United States and European Union markets for fruit and vegetables. FAO Commodity Studies 3. Rome: FAO. Retrieved from http://www.fao.org/3/a-a1245e.pdf (last accessed October 2019).

Department for Environment Food and Rural Affairs (2017). UK statement on sustainable palm oil: Final progress report. London: DEFRA. Retrieved from https://assets

.publishing.service.gov.uk/government/uploads/system/uploads/attachment_data/ file/590473/palm-oil-final-report.pdf (last accessed December 2019).

Dingwerth, K. and Pattberg, P. (2009). World politics and organizational fields: The case of transnational sustainability governance. *European Journal of International Relations* 15(4), 707–44, doi: 10.1177/1354066109345056.

Friends of the Earth International (2009). "Certified" palm oil not a solution. Retrieved from   https://www.foei.org/press_releases/archive-by-subject/food-sovereignty -press/certified-palm-oil-not-a-solution (last accessed December 2019).

Giessen, L., Burns, S., Sahide, M.A.K. and Wibowo, A. (2016). From governance to government: The strength and role of state bureaucracies in forest and agricultural certification. *Politics and Society* 35(1), 71–89, doi: 10.1016/j.polsoc.2016.02.001.

GLOBALG.A.P. (2019). GLOBALG.A.P. General regulations: Part II—quality management system rules. English version 5.2. Cologne: GLOBALG.A.P. Retrieved from   https://www.globalgap.org/.content/.galleries/documents/190201_GG_GR _Part-II_V5_2_en.pdf (last accessed June 2020).

Gnych, S.M., Limberg, G. and Paoli, G. (2015). Risky business: Motivating uptake and implementation of sustainability standards in the Indonesian palm oil sector. Occasional Paper 139. Bogor, Indonesia: Centre for International Forestry Research. Retrieved from https://www.cifor.org/library/5748/ (last accessed January 2020).

Harsono, D., Chozin, M.A. and Fauzi, A.M. (2012). Analysis on Indonesian sustainable palm oil (ISPO): A qualitative assessment of the success factors for ISPO. *Jurnal Manajmen & Agribisnis* 9, 39–48.

Henson, S. and Humphrey, J. (2010). Understanding the complexities of private standards in global agri-food chains as they impact developing countries. *Journal of Development Studies* 46(9), 1628–46, doi: 10.1080/00220381003706494.

Hidayat, N.K., Offermans, A. and Glasbergen, P. (2018). Sustainable palm oil as a public responsibility? On the governance capacity of Indonesian standard for sustainable palm oil (ISPO). *Agriculture and Human Values* 35, 223–42, doi: 10.1007/ s10460-017-9816-6.

Hidayat, R.A. (2018). The implementation of Indonesian sustainable palm oil (ISPO) and SDGs. Presentation made at 14th Indonesian Palm Oil Conference (IPOC), Bali, October.

Hospes, O. (2014). Marking the success or end of global multi-stakeholder governance? The rise of national sustainability standards in Indonesia and Brazil for palm oil and soy. *Agriculture and Human Values* 31(3), 425–37, doi: 10.1007/ s10460-014-9511-9.

Hughes, A. (2001). Multi-stakeholder approaches to ethical trade: Towards a reorganisation of UK retailers' global supply chains? *Journal of Economic Geography* 1(4), 421–37, doi: 10.1093/jeg/1.4.421.

Humphrey, J. (2008). Private standards, small farmers and donor policy: EUREPGAP in Kenya. IDS Working Paper 308. Brighton: Institute of Development Studies. Retrieved from http://www.ids.ac.uk/files/Wp308.pdf (last accessed June 2018).

Humphrey, J. (2017). Regulation, standards, and risk management in the context of globalisation. In E. Michida, J. Humphrey and K. Nabeshima (eds), *Regulations and International Trade: New Sustainability Challenges for East Asia*. Basingstoke: Palgrave Macmillan, pp. 21–58.

Hutabarat, S. (2017). ISPO certification and Indonesian palm oil competitiveness in global market: Smallholder challenges toward ISPO certification. *Agro Ekonomi* 28(2), 170–88.

Hutabarat, S., Slingerland, M., Rietberg, P. and Dries, L. (2018). Costs and benefits of certification of independent oil palm smallholders in Indonesia. *International Food and Agribusiness Management Review* 21(6), 681–700, doi: 10.22434/IFAMR2016.0162.

Hutabarat, S., Slingerland, M. and Dries, L. (2019). Explaining the "certification gap" for different types of oil palm smallholders in Riau Province, Indonesia. *Journal of Environment & Development* 28(3), 253–81, doi: 10.1177/1070496519854505.

IDH and Solidaridad (2020). National initiatives for sustainable & climate smart oil palm smallholders (NI-SCOPS). The Hague: IDH and Solidaridad. Retrieved from https://www.idhsustainabletrade.com/uploaded/2019/12/20190508-3-pager -NI-SCOPS.pdf (last accessed June 2020).

ISO (2010). International standards and "private standards" ISO/TC 34 SC17. Geneva: International Organisation for Standardisation. Retrieved from http://www.iso.org/iso/private_standards.pdf (last accessed July 2012).

Jelsma, I., Schoneveld, G.C., Zoomers, A. and van Westen, A.C.M. (2017). Unpacking Indonesia's independent oil palm smallholders: An actor-disaggregated approach to identifying environmental and social performance challenges. *Land Use Policy* 69, 281–97, doi: 10.1016/j.landusepol.2017.08.012.

Jong, H.N. (2018). Small farmers not ready as Indonesia looks to impose its palm oil sustainability standard on all. Retrieved from https://news.mongabay.com/2018/04/small-farmers-not-ready-as-indonesia-looks-to-impose-its-palm-oil-sustainability -standard-on-all/ (last accessed October 2019).

Jong, H.N. (2020). Indonesia aims for sustainability certification for oil palm small-holders. Retrieved from https://news.mongabay.com/2020/04/indonesia-aims-for -sustainability-certification-for-oil-palm-smallholders/ (last accessed June 2020).

Junginger, M., Koppejan, J. and Goh, C.S. (2020). Sustainable bioenergy deployment in East and South East Asia: Notes on recent trends. *Sustainability Science* 15(3), 1455–9, doi: 10.1007/s11625-019-00712-w.

Kadarusman, Y.B. and Pramudya, E.P. (2019). The effects of India and China on the sustainability of palm oil production in Indonesia: Towards a better understanding of the dynamics of regional sustainability governance. *Sustainable Development* 27(5), 898–909, doi: 10.1002/sd.1949.

Kailany, M.N. (2011). Smallholders in Malaysia. Presentation made at the 9th Annual Roundtable Meeting on Sustainable Palm Oil, Sabah Borneo, November. Retrieved from http://rt9.rspo.org/ckfinder/userfiles/files/P7_6_Mohd_Nor_Kailany.pdf (last accessed October 2019).

Kuntom, A. (2016). MSPO implementation and voluntary schemes in Malaysia. Presentation made at ISCC Technical Committee South East Asia Fifth Meeting, Bali.

Kuntom, A. (2018). Cooperation between smallholder groups and the industry to build an efficient mechanism for certification. International Palm Oil Sustainability Conference 2018, Kota Kinabalu. Retrieved from http://www.mpoc.org.my/upload/Paper-6-IPOSC-2018-Dr-Ainie-Kuntom.pdf (last accessed October 2019).

Malaysian Palm Oil Certification Council (MPOCC) (2018). Combined audit checklist (MSPO and RSPO p&c—myni).

Malaysian Palm Oil Certification Council (MPOCC) (2019). Standards review: Announcement. Retrieved from https://www.mpocc.org.my/standards-review (last accessed June 2020).

McInnes, A. (2017). A comparison of leading palm oil certification standards. Moreton-in-Marsh: Forest Peoples Programme. Retrieved from http://www .forestpeoples.org/sites/default/files/documents/Palm%20Oil%20Certification %20Standards_lowres_spreads.pdf (last accessed June 2018).

Ministry of Agriculture of the Republic of Indonesia, S. o. t. I. S. P. O. I. C. (2015). Joint study on the similarities and differences of the ISPO and the RSPO certification systems. Jakarta: United Nations Development Programme (UNDP), Sustainable Palm Oil Initiative (SPOI). Retrieved from https://www.undp.org/content/dam/ gp-commodities/docs/ISPO-RSPO%20Joint%20Study_English_N%208%20for %20screen.pdf (last accessed June 2020).

Nikoloyuk, J., Burns, T.R. and de Man, R. (2010). The promise and limitations of partner governance: The case of sustainable palm oil. *Corporate Governance* 10(1), 59–72, doi: 10.1108/14720701011021111.

OECD (2006). Final report on private standards and the shaping of the agro-food system AGR/CA/APM(2006)9/FINAL. Paris: OECD, Directorate for Food, Agriculture and Fisheries, Committee for Agriculture. Retrieved from http://www.oecd.org/ officialdocuments/publicdisplaydocumentpdf/?cote=AGR/CA/APM(2006)9/ FINAL&docLanguage=En (last accessed October 2019).

Ouma, S. (2010). Global standards, local realities: Private agri-food governance and the restructuring of the Kenyan horticulture industry. *Economic Geography* 86(2), 197–222, doi: 10.1111/j.1944-8287.2009.01065.x.

Pacheco, P., Schoneveld, G., Dermawan, A., Komarudin, H. and Djama, M. (2020). Governing sustainable palm oil supply: Disconnects, complementarities, and antagonisms between state regulations and private standards. *Regulation & Governance* 14(3), 568–98, doi: 10.1111/rego.12220.

Pramudya, E.P., Hospes, O. and Termeer, C.J.A.M. (2018). Friend or foe? The various responses of the Indonesian state to sustainable non-state palm oil initiatives. *Asian Journal of Sustainability and Social Responsibility* 3(1), 1–22, doi: 10.1186/ s41180-018-0018-y.

Rahman, N.K. (2016). MSPO certification: Implementation of smallholders challenges. Presentation made at ISCC Regional Stakeholders Dialogue, Cititel Penang. Retrieved from https://www.iscc-system.org/wp-content/uploads/2017/ 05/12.-Khabibor_Rahman_MPOB_ISCC_Technical_Committee_061216.pdf (last accessed January 2020).

Roozen, N. (2018). Palm oil allows millions to escape from poverty. Retrieved from https://www.mapa-solidaridad.org/post/palm-oil-allows-millions-to-escape-from -poverty (last accessed June 2020).

Rosniza Aznie, C.R., Lyndon, N., Yaakob, M.J. et al. (2018). Independent oil palm smallholders' challenges in Malaysia. *International Journal of Academic Research in Business & Social Sciences* 8(13), 68–75, doi: 10.6007/IJARBSS/v8-i13/4810.

Roundtable on Sustainable Palm Oil (2007). RSPO principles and criteria for sustainable palm oil production: Including indicators and guidance. Retrieved from https:// www.rspo.org/file/RSPO%20Principles%20&%20Criteria%20Document.pdf (last accessed November 2020).

Roundtable on Sustainable Palm Oil (2018). RSPO impact report 2018. Kuala Lumpur: RSPO Secretariat. Retrieved from https://rspo.org/key-documents/impact-reports (last accessed January 2020).

Sahide, M.A.K., Burns, S., Wibowo, A., Nurrochmat, D.R. and Giessen, L. (2015). Towards state hegemony over agricultural certification: From voluntary private to mandatory state regimes on palm oil in Indonesia. *Journal of Tropical Forest Management* 21(3), 162–71, doi: 10.7226/jtfm.21.3.162.

Schleifer, P. and Sun, Y. (2018). Emerging markets and private governance: The political economy of sustainable palm oil in China and India. *Review of International Political Economy* 25(2), 190–214, doi: 10.1080/09692290.2017.1418759.

Schoneveld, G.C., van der Haar, S., Ekowati, D. et al. (2019). Certification, good agricultural practice and smallholder heterogeneity: Differentiated pathways for resolving compliance gaps in the Indonesian oil palm sector. *Global Environmental Change*, 57, 1–18, doi: 10.1016/j.gloenvcha.2019.101933.

Senawi, R., Rahman, N.K., Mansor, N. and Kuntom, A. (2019). Transformation of oil palm independent smallholders through Malaysian sustainable palm oil. *Journal of Oil Palm Research* 31, 496–507, doi: 10.21894/jopr.2019.0038.

Solidaridad (2018). Indonesian and Indian palm oil industry join hands to promote sustainable trade. Retrieved from https://www.solidaridadnetwork.org/news/indonesian -indian-palm-oil-industry-join-hands-to-promote-sustainable-trade (last accessed October 2019).

Stockholm Environment Institute (2019). Perspectives on sustainability—making supply chains work for smallholders. Stockholm: Stockholm Environment Institute. Retrieved from https://www.sei.org/wp-content/uploads/2019/03/sei-2019-p2cs -palm-oil-sustainability-smallholders.pdf (last accessed October 2019).

Swinnen, J. and Kuijpers, R. (2019). The governance of global agri-food value chains, standards and development. In E. Brousseau, J.-M. Glachant and J. Sgard (eds), *The Oxford Handbook of Institutions of International Economic Governance and Market Regulation*. Oxford: Oxford University Press, pp. 1–29.

Teoh, C.H. (2010). Key sustainability issues in the palm oil sector: A discussion paper for multi-stakeholders consultations. Washington, DC: World Bank. Retrieved from http://siteresources.worldbank.org/INTINDONESIA/Resources/226271 -1170911056314/Discussion.Paper_palmoil.pdf (last accessed December 2019).

Teoh, C.H. (2011). Spearheading development & promotion of sustainable palm oil in China. Roundtable on Sustainable Palm 9, Sabah. Retrieved from http://rt9.rspo.org/ ckfinder/userfiles/files/P1_3_Teoh_Cheng_Hai.pdf (last accessed November 2020).

Vis, J.K., Teoh, C.H., Chandran, M.R., Diemer, M., Lord, S. and McIntosh, I. (2012). Sustainable development of palm oil industry. In O.-M. Lai, C.-P. Tan and C.C. Akoh (eds), *Palm Oil: Production, Processing, Characterization, and Uses*. Urbana, AOCS, pp. 737–83.

Vogel, D. (2010). The private regulation of global corporate conduct: Achievements and limitations. *Business & Society* 49(1), 68–87, doi: 10.1177/0007650309343407.

von Hagen, O. and Alvarez, G. (2011). The impact of private standards on global value chains. Literature Review Series on the Impacts of Private Standards; Part I. Geneva: ITC. Retrieved from http://www.intracen.org/the-impacts-of-private-standards-on -global-value-chains-literature-review-series-on-the-impacts-of-private-standards/ (last accessed November 2015).

Watts, J.D. and Irawan, S. (2018). Oil palm in Indonesia. LEAVES Background Paper. Washington, DC: World Bank. Retrieved from https://www.profor.info/sites/profor .info/files/Oil%20Palm_Case%20Study_LEAVES_2018.pdf (last accessed October 2019).

Wijaya, A. and Glasbergen, P. (2016). Toward a new scenario in agricultural sustainability certification? The response of the Indonesian national government to private certification. *Journal of Environment & Development* 25(2), 219–46, doi: 10.1177/1070496516640857.

WTO (2007). Private standards and the SPS agreement, note by the secretariat G/SPS/ GEN/746. Geneva: WTO, Committee on Sanitary and Phytosanitary Measures. Retrieved from http://www.wto.org/english/docs_e/docs_e.htm (last accessed July 2012).

WWF (2012). Profitability and sustainability in palm oil production. Washington, DC: World Wildlife Fund. Retrieved from https://wwf.panda.org/?204548/Profitability -and-Sustainability-in-Palm-Oil-Production (last accessed December 2019).

3. Factors explaining the adoption of green building rating systems at the country level: competition of LEED and other green building rating systems

Kenji Shiraishi and Hajime Iseda

3.1 INTRODUCTION

Climate change mitigation is widely recognized as one of the pressing challenges of the 21st century. Lowering greenhouse gas (GHG) emissions is vital in mitigating climate change. One of the critical pillars in lowering GHG emissions worldwide is to lower GHG emissions from the building sector. The building sector contributes approximately 30% of global GHG emissions and consumes about 40% of global energy (Lucon et al., 2014), making it one of the largest shares of GHG emissions and primary energy consumption in many industrial countries. Thus, the need for creating and stimulating the development of economically, environmentally, and socially sustainable buildings, commonly referred to as "green buildings," is increasing throughout the world (Asensio and Delmas, 2017; Hoffert et al., 2002).

While there are a variety of ways to describe green buildings, they are usually certified by one or more rating systems. These rating systems provide standards to verify which buildings can be appropriately described as "green." Today, these standards are mostly voluntary (Zou et al., 2017). Unlike government regulations, which are mandatory and domestic by nature, voluntary rating systems are voluntary and can be used internationally. For the past ten years or so, LEED (Leadership in Energy and Environmental Design), which was developed in the United States, has been one of the leading rating systems for sustainable design and construction in the United States as well as globally (Accame et al., 2012). LEED-certified buildings have been developed in more than 115 countries and LEED Accredited Professionals (LEED AP) work in 136 countries (as of November 2018). However, over the past few decades, alternative rating systems have also been developed. This is because systems used globally may not be suitable for the specific situations on the ground (Alyami et al., 2015). Despite the growing number of alternative rating systems, research has placed more focus on LEED implementation and has disregarded the development and diffusion of other green building rating systems worldwide (Darko et al., 2019). The World Green Building Council in 2017 called for more attention to be paid to country- or context-specific green building rating systems. This would provide a closer insight into the different characteristics of each place, leading to the most appropriate fit of rating system to specific locations.

Voluntary rating systems for green buildings have made particularly important contributions to promoting the practice of green building for the following reasons. First, voluntary rating systems can encourage the design and development of innovative and high-quality green buildings when compared with the outcomes resulting from mandatory laws such as energy efficiency codes for buildings. Due to its mandatory nature, building codes tend to be "minimum standards," which does not encourage innovative green building practices. At the same time, stringent energy efficiency codes for buildings are difficult to introduce in developing countries due to their economic and technical capacity. Second, the voluntary nature of such rating systems encourages wider spread on a faster timeline across the world. Voluntary rating systems for green buildings have been rapidly introduced, encouraging capacity building and technology transfer on green buildings, as shown in the next chapter. Because building stocks with poor energy efficiency can exist for several decades (or more), the earlier green buildings can be developed the longer lasting the beneficial effect on mitigating global climate change. Lastly, voluntary rating systems can be used as a substitute for mandatory standards in states and countries where expertise on green building is limited; creating reliable standards requires technical and scientific expertise, efforts, and funding. Established voluntary rating systems, therefore, could work as a reliable source of information and be legalized in various states in the United States.

In 2001, Japan created its voluntary rating system called the CASBEE (Comprehensive Assessment System for Built Environment Efficiency), and, as of March 2016, has certified over 18,552 green buildings throughout the country. However, despite the governments' efforts to have CASBEE adoptable outside of Japan, to date, only one project in China has used the system. If we take the case of Japan, we see that while a country-specific green building rating system may increase the number of green buildings in that country, it may not be capable of increasing the number of green buildings globally. Taking into account that eliminating GHG emissions is a global task and investing in green buildings, especially in non-OECD countries, is crucial to lowering GHG emissions, clarifying the relationship between domestically developed rating systems (which are increasing in number) and globally uti-lized rating systems within each country is an important area of study. There has been research comparing globally and domestically used rating systems across countries (Doan et al., 2017; Mattoni et al., 2018) but not between different rating systems within countries.

The purpose of this research is exploratory on the following research ques-tions. Is it cost-effective for a country to create a rating system relevant to its own individual characteristics in this globalized market economy? What is the relationship between domestically created rating systems and globally used rating systems within the same country? Why do some rating systems coexist within a country while others don't? Taking into account the tendencies examined, we will conclude by discussing the benefits and costs of developing a country-specific standard in a global market society.

3.2   EMPIRICAL STUDIES

This study used country-level data to examine how the competition of green building rating systems affects the development of LEED-certified buildings in each country. Based on our literature review, we controlled for the environ-mental, economic, and social variables that are hypothesized to contribute to the development of green buildings.

The number of LEED-certified buildings is specified as a function of the dummy variable of domestic green building rating systems of the country and a set of economic, climate, and social variables:

$$E[L_c|R_c, X_c] = exp[\beta R_c + ln(P\ op_c) + X_c\gamma] \tag{3.1}$$

where L_c represents the number of LEED-certified buildings in country c, R_c the dummy variable of green building rating systems in country c, $P\ op_c$ the country population (the offset variable). The vector X_c includes economic, climate, and social variables explained in detail in the following section addressing independent variables.

Because the dependent variable takes integer values, we employed a neg-ative binomial regression for coefficient estimation. We also tested and con-firmed the overdispersion of the residuals of the Poisson regression. Therefore, negative binomial regression is more appropriate for statistical inference than Poisson regression in this study.

3.2.1   Dependent Variables

The dependent variable of this study was total number of LEED-certified projects per capita in a given country. Data on LEED-certified projects and accredited professionals (AP) were collected from the LEED website. As of February 2018, 74,062 certified projects and 64,599 accredited professionals were registered on the LEED website. Country-level datasets were created from the data.

3.2.2   Independent Variables

3.2.2.1   Competing green building rating system
The coexistence of domestic green building rating systems other than LEED is hypothesized to hinder adoption of the LEED rating system. This is because the countries' governments, industries, and professionals have strong incentives to use their own rating system instead. We used the list of green building rating systems around the world, created by the World Green Building Council. Table 3.1 summarizes the list of green building rating systems and the countries where they are developed.

Table 3.1   List of green building rating systems

Rating Name	Country
BEAM Plus	Hong Kong
BOMA Best	Canada
BREEAM	UK, Netherlands, Spain, Norway, Germany, Sweden
CASA	Brazil
Casa	Columbia
CASBEE	Japan
DGNB	Germany
EcoProfile	Norway
GBC	Italy
GBEL	China
Green Building Certification	South Korea
Green Building Guideline	Pakistan
Green Building Index	Malaysia
Green Mark	Singapore
Green SL	Sri Lanka
Green Star	Australia
Green Star SA	South Africa
HQE	France
LOTUS	Vietnam
PEARL	United Arab Emirates (UAE)
Verde	Sweden

Source: Author created from the website of World Green Building Council.

3.2.2.2   Other independent variables

The existing literature showed that green buildings are geographically clustered and that there are physical, economic, social, and policy factors that influence this clustering. In order to control such factors, we include the following variables as independent variables in the statistical model.

First, each country's average temperature and its squared term serves as a proxy for environmental condition. Deviation from comfortable average temperature is expected to contribute to the development of more energy efficient buildings. We included the squared term so that we can account for the deviation with quadratic function of the average temperature. The data on average temperature by country, from 1961 to 1999, were downloaded from the World Bank (World Bank Website).

Second, two economic variables, gross domestic product (GDP) per capita (constant 2010 US$) and energy use (kg of oil equivalent per capita) in 2015, were obtained from the World Development Index (WDI). GDP per capita is employed as the proxy for a country's economic condition. A strong economy is considered as one of the major drivers of the adoption of green buildings rating systems. On the other hand, high per capita energy consumption also has considerable potential as an economic incentive to invest in green buildings.

Third, urban population (% of total) was obtained from the WDI and employed as a proxy for the degree of urbanization. Urbanization contributes to the demand for the construction of new buildings.

Fourth, information about public policies associated with green buildings was derived from climate policy data downloaded from the Climate Policy Database (Climate Policy Database Website). These data identified those countries with at least one policy relating to green buildings.

Finally, the number of international students in the United States by place of origin is employed as a proxy for the knowledge flow between the country and the United States. The data on the number of international students by place of

Table 3.2   Summary statistics (n = 193)

	Min.	1st Qu.	Median	Mean	3rd Qu.	Max.
Number of LEED-certified buildings	0	0	1	29.88	12	925
Average temperature (Celsius)	-7.15	10.51	22.19	18.56	25.11	28.3
GDP per capita (constant 2010 US$; thousands)	213	2 024	6376	14 887	17 885	107 865
Urban population (% of total)	12.71	41.37	61.30	60.11	79.84	100.00
Number of international students in the US	0	10	333	4 692	1 563	350 755
Population (thousands)	11	1 431	7 392	38 080	28 540	1 386 000

origin, 2016/17 and 2017/18 are downloaded from Open Doors of the Institute of International Education (Open Doors: International Students by Place of Origin, 2018).

Table 3.2 shows the summary statistics of the dependent and independent variables.

3.2.3   Comparison of Four Major Rating Systems

After the statistical analysis, we compared four major green building rating systems—LEED (US), Building Research Establishment Environmental Assessment Method (BREEAM) (UK and other European countries), CASBEE (Japan), and Green Star (Australia)—and discussed the interpretation of the results of the statistical analysis. As shown in the results section, CASBEE and Green Star have statistically significant negative association with the number of LEED buildings, after controlling other covariates. On the other hand, BREEAM, the second most widely used green building rating system around the world after LEED, did not have statistically significant association with the number of LEED buildings. By comparing the similarities of these rating systems with LEED, we intended to draw insights of voluntary domestic rating system design in the existence of de facto international voluntary rating systems.

It is not easy or simple to compare voluntary rating systems, because their reference guides are typically hundreds of pages long and include detailed information for each evaluation criterion. For example, the New Building certification requirements are about 800 pages for LEED (v4 BD + C), and 500 pages for BREEAM. Knowledge, skill, and practical experience is required to understand and identify the nuanced variations between the similar criteria. Therefore, in order to quantitatively and objectively calculate the similarities between different guidelines, we counted the number of same evaluation criteria of each rating system against that of LEED and calculated the percentage of such evaluation criteria of other rating systems to all evaluation criteria as similarity. We calculated both simple similarity and point-weighted similarity.

3.3   RESULTS AND DISCUSSION

3.3.1   Regression Results

As discussed above, equation (3.1) is employed to test whether there is any statistically significant association between the identified factors and the adoption of LEED-certified buildings at the country level.

Based on equation (3.1), we constructed three models with different combinations of independent variables. Model (1) controlled for rating system R_c to examine the variation in the owner countries of green building rating systems. Model (2) additionally controlled for social and policy variables. Table 3.3 reports the results obtained in the empirical estimations, which employ the number of LEED-certified buildings per capita as the dependent variable.

Table 3.3   Regression results

	Coefficients (SD)	
Variables	Model (1)	Model (2)
BEAM Plus (Hong Kong)	1.955 (1.951)	0.236 (1.513)
BOMA Best/Green Globe (Canada)	2.623 (1.948)	2.155 (1.804)
BREEAM (UK, Netherlands, Spain, Germany, Norway, Sweden)	-0.131 (0.991)	-1.126 (0.826)
CASA (Brazil)	-0.176 (1.949)	-0.950 (1.489)
Casa (Columbia)	-0.405 (1.953)	-0.740 (1.488)
CASBEE (Japan)	-1.443 (1.954)	-3.148 (1.517) *
DGNB (Germany)	0.472 (2.175)	0.698 (1.666)
GBC (Italy)	0.012 (1.951)	-0.147 (1.499)
GBEL (China)	-1.074 (1.983)	-4.724 (3.055)
Green Building Certification (South Korea)	0.433 (1.950)	-0.136 (1.494)
Green Building Guideline (Pakistan)	-3.448 (1.976)	-1.461 (1.519)
Green Building Index (Malaysia)	-0.102 (1.954)	-0.101 (1.527)
Green SL (Sri Lanka)	2.588 (1.514)	2.588 (1.514)
Green Mark (Singapore)	1.742 (1.953)	-0.741 (1.534)
Green Star (Australia)	-1.521 (1.449)	-2.990 (1.197) *
Green Star SA (South Africa)	-2.454 (1.984)	-1.970 (1.527)
HQE (France)	-1.273 (1.957)	-2.134 (1.511)
LOTUS (Vietnam)	-2.149 (1.964)	-0.020 (1.499)
PEARL (UAE)	3.996 (1.948) *	2.637 (1.509)
Verde (Sweden)	1.603 (2.177)	1.536 (1.685)
Average temperature		0.069 (0.068)
Average temperature squared		-0.0016 (0.0022)
GDP per capita (constant 2010 US$; thousands)		0.026 (0.0094) **
Urban population (% of total)		0.049 (0.0072) ***

Table 3.3 (continued)   Regression results

	Coefficients (SD)	
Green building policy		-0.192 (0.368)
Number of international students in the US per thousand people		0.014 (0.007)
Constant	-13.45 (0.162) ***	-18.10 (0.664) ***
Observations	193	193
Log Likelihood	-550.6	-511.5
θ	0.2654 (0.0309) ***	0.4682 (0.0617) ***
AIC	1147.1	1081.2

Note: * $p < 0.05$, ** $p < 0.01$, *** $p < 0.001$.

Model (1) controlled for the green rating systems of each country. Likelihood ratio tests of negative binomial models show that its Likelihood ratio against the null model is 57.75266; this model is significant at 0.1% level with pseudo R^2 of 0.153.

Model (2) controlled all covariates in addition to the green rating systems. Both AIC and pseudo R^2 improved; Model (2)'s AIC is 1082.1, while that of Model (1) is 1147.1; Model (2)'s pseudo R^2 is 0.464 against that of Model (1) of 0.153. Controlling the other independent variables, the existence of competing standards is associated with the significant decrease in the adoption of LEED in the scheme owner countries of those standards. Of the green building ratings, Japan's CASBEE and Australia's Green Star showed statistically significant association with the decrease in the number of LEED-certified buildings at 5% level. Other green building ratings, including BREEAM, did not show significant association with it. Of the other independent variables, GDP per capita and urban population also showed statistical significance at 5% level. On the other hand, average temperature, its squared term, green building policy, and number of international students in the United States did not show evidence for the association with the number of LEED-certified buildings.

Table 3.4 shows the percent change of LEED building when each variable changes by one standard deviation for quantitative variables or by the dummy variables for qualitative variables (i.e. CASBEE and Green Star), holding other variables constant. Urban population and GDP per capita have strong and statistically significant positive influence on the adoption of LEED-certified buildings, while CASBEE and Green Star have statistically significant negative influence on the development of LEED-certified buildings. In addition to statistical significance, the magnitude of the negative effect of CASBEE and Green Star are particularly high; controlling all other variables, LEED-certified buildings in Japan and Australia are less than 10% of the reference level.

In the next section, we examined why the coefficients, or influence of BREEAM, CASBEE, and Green Star on the adoption of LEED-certified buildings are so different, by comparing the guidelines of the rating systems with that of LEED.

Table 3.4   Percent change in the number of LEED-certified buildings with one standard deviation change from the mean

Variables	Mean	One SD	% change	p-value
GDP per capita (constant 2010 US$; thousands)	14.74	19.79	67.5	0.006
Urban population (% of total)	60.06	23.59	214.9	0.000
CASBEE (Japan)	–	–	-95.7	0.038
Green Star (Australia)	–	–	-95.0	0.001

3.3.2   Discussion and Policy Implications

As shown above, when controlling relevant covariates, while there are a significantly smaller number of LEED-certified buildings in Japan and Australia, where CASBEE and Green Star originated, the effect of BREEAM on the development of LEED was not statistically significant. We examined the similarity of the guidelines of LEED, BREEAM, CASBEE, and Green Star to understand the regression results.

3.3.2.1   BREEAM and LEED

First, we compared the contents and options of the LEED Reference Guide for Building Design and Construction version 4 [9] with BREEAM International New Building 2016—Technical Manual SD 233 2.0. Some scoring options typically differ with the building type and scale, even within the same rating system; therefore, an office building was used as a case study. This study is only concerned with comparing the credit names, although the programs' difficulty were not compared in detail.

The similarity of BREEAM and LEED was about 90.1% for the credit points and 90.9% between the credit items as shown in Table 3.5. The most different items can be categorized into three types. First is "cost," which includes building management ("Management 02" in the guideline). Second is "resilience for the future," which involves "Health and Wellbeing 04" and "Waste 05." The third is "others." It is noted that LEED does not directly reward points for cost reduction unlike BREEAM, except for some items in materials and resources. Also, LEED does not count resilience measures against future climate changes unlike BREEAM. For the "others" category, elevators and escalators are not explicitly rated in the LEED system, but instead can be accounted for under the Optimize Energy Performance category. Water quality is not included in the LEED credit points because it is regulated by US law.

Table 3.5　The similarity of BREEAM and LEED

| BREEAM | | | LEED | |
Categories and Contents	Max Points	Points		Categories and Contents
Management 01 Project brief and design				
Stakeholder consultation (project delivery)	4	1	IP	Integrative design charrette
Stakeholder consultation (third party)		1	IN	LEED Accredited Professional
Sustainability champion (design)		1	EA	Enhanced Commissioning
Sustainability champion (monitoring progress)		1		
Management 02 Life cycle cost and service life planning				
Elemental life cycle cost (LCC)	4	2		
Component level LCC options appraisal		1		
Capital cost reporting				
Management 03 Responsible construction practices				
Legally harvested and traded timber	6	Pre	MR	Building Product Disclosure and Optimization —Environmental Product Declarations
National health and safety legislation		Pre	EQ	Construction Indoor Air Quality Management Plan
Environmental management		1	EQ	Construction Indoor Air Quality Management Plan
Sustainability champion (construction)		1		
Considerate construction		Up to two	MR	Construction and Demolition Waste Management Planning
Monitoring of site impacts		Up to two	MR	Storage and Collection of Recyclables
Management 04 Commissioning and handover				
Commissioning and testing schedule and responsibilities	4	1	EA	Fundamental Commissioning and Verification Enhanced Commissioning
Commissioning building services		1	EA	Fundamental Commissioning and Verification Enhanced Commissioning
Testing and inspecting building fabric		1	EA	Fundamental Commissioning and Verification Enhanced Commissioning
Handover		1	EA	Fundamental Commissioning and Verification Enhanced Commissioning
Management 05 Aftercare				
Aftercare support	3	1	EA	Fundamental Commissioning and Verification Enhanced Commissioning
Seasonal commissioning		1	EA	Fundamental Commissioning and Verification Enhanced Commissioning
Post-occupancy evaluation (POE)		1	EA	Fundamental Commissioning and Verification Enhanced Commissioning

BREEAM Categories and Contents	Max Points	Points	LEED code	LEED Categories and Contents
Health and wellbeing 01 Visual comfort	6			
High frequency ballasts		Pre	EA	Optimize Energy Performance
Glare control		1	EQ	Daylight
Daylighting (building type dependent)		Up to four	EQ	Daylight
View out		1	EQ	Quality Views
Internal and external lighting levels, zoning and control		1	EQ	Interior Lighting
Health and wellbeing 02 Indoor air quality	5			
Avoidance of asbestos		Pre	MR	Building Life-Cycle Impact Reduction
Indoor air quality (IAQ) plan		1	EQ	Minimum Indoor Air Quality Performance
Ventilation		1	EQ	Minimum Indoor Air Quality Performance
Emissions from building products		1	EQ	Low-Emitting Materials
Post-construction indoor air quality measurement		1	EQ	Indoor Air Quality Assessment
Adaptability - Potential for natural ventilation		1	EQ	Minimum Indoor Air Quality Performance
Health and wellbeing 04 Thermal comfort	3			
Thermal modelling		1	EQ	Thermal Comfort
Adaptability for a projected climate change scenario		1		Thermal Comfort
Thermal zoning and controls		1	EQ	Thermal Comfort
Health and wellbeing 05 Thermal comfort	4			
Suitably qualified acoustician		Pre	EQ	Acoustic Performance
Indoor ambient noise and sound insulation		1	EQ	Acoustic Performance
Health and wellbeing 06 Accessibility	2			
Safe access		1	LT	Access to Quality Transit
Inclusive and accessible design (all buildings except residential)		1		
Health and wellbeing 07 Hazards	1			
Natural hazard		1	LT	Sustainable Site
Health and wellbeing 09 Water quality	1			
Building services water systems		1		
Minimising risk of contamination				
Energy 01 Reduction of energy use and carbon emissions	15			
Option 1 – Use of approved building energy calculation software		Up to 15	EA	Minimum Energy Performance
Option 2 – Energy efficient design features		Up to 10	EA	Optimize Energy Performance
Energy 02a Energy monitoring	2			
Sub-metering of major energy-consuming systems		1	EA	Building-Level Energy Metering
Sub-metering of high energy load and tenancy areas		1	EA	Advanced Energy Metering

Table 3.5 (continued)   *The similarity of BREEAM and LEED*

BREEAM — Categories and Contents	Max Points	Points		LEED — Categories and Contents
Energy 03 External lighting				
Energy efficient light fittings	1	1	EA	Optimize Energy Performance
Energy 04 Low carbon design				
Passive design analysis		1	IP	
Free cooling	3	1	EA	Optimize Energy Performance
		1	EA	Optimize Energy Performance
Low zero carbon feasibility study		1	EA	Green Power and Carbon Offsets
Energy 05 Energy efficient cold storage				
Energy efficient design, installation, and commissioning	3	1	EA	Optimize Energy Performance
				Advanced Energy Metering
Energy efficiency criteria		1	EA	Optimize Energy Performance
Indirect greenhouse gas emissions		1	EA	Enhanced Refrigerant Management
Energy 06 Energy efficient transport systems				
Energy consumption	3	1		
Energy efficient features		2		
Energy 08 Energy efficient equipment				
Energy efficient equipment	2	2	EA	Optimize Energy Performance
Transport 01 Public transport accessibility				
Accessibility Index	5	Up to five	LT	Access to Quality Transit
Transport 02 Proximity to amenities				
Proximity	2	Up to two	LT	Access to Quality Transit
Transport 03a Alternative modes of transport				
Travel using low carbon modes of transport	2	Up to two	LT	Green Vehicles
Transport 04 Maximum car parking capacity				
Car parking capacity	2	Up to two	LT	Reduced Parking Footprint
Transport 05 Travel plan				
Travel assessment	1	1	LT	Access to Quality Transit
Water 01 Water consumption				
Reducing the demand for potable water	5	Up to five	WE	Indoor Water Use Reduction
Water 02 Water monitoring				
Water meters on the mains water supply	1	1	WE	Building-Level Water Metering
Water 03 Water leak detection and prevention				
Leak detection system	3	1	WE	Water Metering
Flow control devices (all buildings except residential)		1	WE	Indoor Water Use Reduction
Water 04 Water efficient equipment				
Reduce water consumption	1	1	WE	Indoor Water Use Reduction

BREEAM				LEED
Categories and Contents	Max Points	Points		Categories and Contents
Materials 01 Life cycle impacts				
LCA	6	1	MR	Building Life-Cycle Impact Reduction
Environmental product declarations (EPD)		1	MR	Building Product Disclosure and Optimization — Environmental Product Declarations
Materials 03 Responsible sourcing of construction products				
All timber and timber-based products	4	Pre	MR	Building Product Disclosure and Optimization —Sourcing of Raw Materials
Sustainable procurement plan		1	MR	Building Product Disclosure and Optimization — Environmental Product Declarations / Building Product Disclosure and Optimization —Sourcing of Raw Materials
Responsible sourcing of construction products		Up to three	MR	Building Product Disclosure and Optimization — Environmental Product Declarations / Building Product Disclosure and Optimization —Sourcing of Raw Materials
Materials 05 Designing for durability and resilience				
Durability and resilience	1	1	MR	Design for Flexibility
Materials 06 Material efficiency				
Optimize material efficiency	1	1	MR	Construction and Demolition Waste Management
Waste 01 Construction waste management				
Construction waste reduction	3	1	MR	Construction and Demolition Waste Management Planning
Construction waste reduction		1	MR	Construction and Demolition Waste Management Planning
Diversion of resources from landfill		1	MR	Construction and Demolition Waste Management Planning
Waste 02 Recycled aggregates				
Recycled aggregates	1	1	MR	Storage and Collection of Recyclables
Waste 03a Operational waste				
Operational waste	1	1	MR	Storage and Collection of Recyclables
Waste 04 Speculative finishes				
Speculative finishes	1	1	MR	Design for Flexibility
Waste 05 Adaptation to climate change				
Adaptation to climate change – structural and fabric resilience	1	1		
Waste 06 Functional adaptability				
Functional adaptability	1	1	MR	Design for Flexibility

Table 3.5 (continued)   The similarity of BREEAM and LEED

BREEAM			LEED	
Categories and Contents	Max Points	Points	Points	Categories and Contents
Management 01 Project brief and design				
Stakeholder consultation (project delivery)	4	1	IP	Integrative design charrette
Stakeholder consultation (third party)		1		
Sustainability champion (design)		1	IN	LEED Accredited Professional
Sustainability champion (monitoring progress)		1	EA	Enhanced Commissioning
Management 02 Life cycle cost and service life planning				
Elemental life cycle cost (LCC)	4	2		
Component level LCC options appraisal		1		
Capital cost reporting		1		
Management 03 Responsible construction practices				
Legally harvested and traded timber		Pre	MR	Building Product Disclosure and Optimization – Environmental Product Declarations
National health and safety legislation		Pre	EQ	Construction Indoor Air Quality Management Plan
Environmental management	6	1	EQ	Construction Indoor Air Quality Management Plan
Sustainability champion (construction)		1		
Considerate construction		Up to two	MR	Construction and Demolition Waste Management Planning
Monitoring of site impacts		Up to two	MR	Storage and Collection of Recyclables
Management 04 Commissioning and handover				
Commissioning and testing schedule and responsibilities		1	EA	Fundamental Commissioning and Verification
Commissioning building services	4	1	EA	Enhanced Commissioning / Fundamental Commissioning and Verification
Testing and inspecting building fabric		1	EA	Enhanced Commissioning / Fundamental Commissioning and Verification
Handover		1	EA	Enhanced Commissioning / Fundamental Commissioning and Verification
Management 05 Aftercare				
Aftercare support		1	EA	Fundamental Commissioning and Verification
Seasonal commissioning	3	1	EA	Enhanced Commissioning / Fundamental Commissioning and Verification
Post-occupancy evaluation (POE)		1	EA	Enhanced Commissioning / Fundamental Commissioning and Verification
Health and wellbeing 01 Visual comfort				
High frequency ballasts	6	Pre	EA	Optimize Energy Performance
Glare control		1	EQ	Daylight
Daylighting (building type dependent)		Up to four	EQ	Daylight
View out		1	EQ	Quality Views
Internal and external lighting levels, zoning and control		1	EQ	Interior Lighting
Health and wellbeing 02 Indoor air quality				

Note: LEED categories: IP: Integrative Process; LT: Location and Transportation; SS: Sustainable Sites; WE: Water Efficiency; EA: Energy and Atmosphere; MR: Material and Resources; EQ: Indoor Environmental Quality; IN: Innovation.

3.3.2.2   CASBEE and LEED

Next, we compared CASBEE for New Construction 2016 version 2.1 [15] with the above-noted LEED guide. Although the BREEAM rating system uses the same point-addition scoring system as LEED, the CASBEE's scoring system is not simple point-addition scoring and is more complex than that of LEED. Therefore, we compared only credit items of CASBEE with that of LEED.

The similarity of CASBEE's credit item with that of LEED was about 51.7% as shown in Table 3.6. In CASBEE, the category with the greatest difference with LEED is Service Efficiency (Q2), which covers a wide range of issues such as functionality, tolerability, reliability, relevancy, and updatability. LEED does not cover such issues. This exclusive category of CASBEE created a significant difference from LEED and resulted in such a low percentage of similarity between the two rating systems.

3.3.2.3   Green Star and LEED

Finally, we compared Green Star of Australia with LEED. The Green Star Design Built version 1.2 (Green Star Website) was used for this research. The Green Star allows users to choose one option among a few options for flexibility. For example, the "Potable Water" metric in Water has more than one option with different score potentials, for example, users could use either option A or B; option A offers ten points, while option B is limited to a maximum of six points. Therefore, comparison of Green Star and LEED is not straightforward. In response, we calculated the maximum and minimum ranges of similarities. When looking at LEED based on the score points of Green Star, the similarities ranged from 52.0% to 81.0% for the score and about 50.0% to 76.3% for the credit list as shown in Table 3.7.

3.3.2.4   The benefit and costs of local green building rating systems

As summarized in Table 3.8, the comparison of the guidelines of four major green building rating systems and regression results indicate that voluntary rating systems with high similarities featured easier adoption by architects, engineers, and other design professionals in foreign markets. Considering the tremendous efforts of the professionals to gain and update the skills and experiences to design and develop certified green buildings under each rating system, each scheme owner of green building standards should be cautious about the similarities of global de facto standards such as LEED and their own domestic rating system. As discussed in the introduction, the major benefit of developing local green building systems that fit their local needs and context is that such local systems could promote the development of green building adoption. However, if the local rating systems are considerably different from the global standards, the local rating system could be a barrier for developing green buildings certified by the global standards as well as a burden on

Table 3.6   The similarity of CASBEE and LEED

CASBEE			LEED	
Categories & Contents			Categories	Contents
Q1 Indoor Environment				
1	Noise & Acoustics		EQ	Acoustic Performance
1.1	Noise & Acoustics			
	Sound Insulation			
1.2	1	Sound Insulation of Openings		
	2	Sound Insulation of Partition Walls		
	3	Sound Insulation Performance of Floor Slabs (light-weight impact source)		
	4	Sound Insulation Performance of Floor Slabs (heavy-weight impact source)		
1.3	Sound Absorption			
	Room Temperature Control			
2.1	1	Room Temperature Setting	EQ	Thermal Comfort
	2	Perimeter Performance	EA	Optimize Energy Performance
	3	Zoned Control	EQ	Thermal Comfort
2.2	Humidity Contorol		EQ	Thermal Comfort
2.3	Type of Air Conditioning System		EQ	Thermal Comfort
	Daylighting			
3.1	1	Daylight Factor	EQ	Daylight
	2	Openings by Orientation	IN	
	3	Daylight Devices	EA	Optimize Energy Performance
3.2	Anti-glare Measures		EQ	Daylight
3.3	Illuminance Level		EQ	Interior Lighting
3.4	Lighting Controllability		EQ	Interior Lighting

CASBEE		LEED	
Categories& Contents		**Categories**	**Contents**
4.1	Source Control		
	1 Chemical Pollutants	EA	Low-Emitting Materials
	2 Asbestos	MR	Building Life Cycle Impact Reduction
4.2	Ventilation		
	1 Ventilation Rate	EQ	Minimum Indoor Air Quality Performance
	2 Natural Ventilation Performance	EQ	Enhanced Indoor Air Quality Strategies
	3 Consideration for Outside Air Intake	EQ	Enhanced Indoor Air Quality Strategies
4.3	Operation Plan		
	1 CO2 Monitoring	EQ	Enhanced Indoor Air Quality Strategies
	2 Control of Smoking		
Q2 Quality of Service			
1.1	Functionality & Usability		
	1 Provision of Space & Storage		
	2 Use of Advanced Information System		
	3 Barrier-free Planning		
1.2	Amenity		
	1 Perceived Spaciousness & Access to View	EQ	Quality View
	2 Space for Refreshment		
	3 Décor Planning	EQ	Interior Lighting
1.3	Maintenance Management		
	1 Design Which Considers Maintenance Management		
	2 Securing Maintenance Management Functions		
2.1	Earthquake Resistance		
	1 Earthquake-resistance		
	2 Seismic Isolation & Vibration Damping Systems		

Table 3.6 (continued)   The similarity of CASBEE and LEED

CASBEE			LEED	
	Categories & Contents		Categories	Contents
Q2 Quality of Service				
	Service Life of Components			
	1	Service Life of Structural Frame Materials	MR	Building Life Cycle Impact Reduction
	2	Necessary Refurbishment Interval for Exterior Finishes		
	3	Necessary Renewal Interval for Main Interior Finishes		
2.2	4	Necessary Replacement Interval for Air Conditioning and Ventilation Ducts		
	5	Necessary Renewal Interval for HVAC and Water Supply and Drainage Pipes		
	6	Necessary Renewal Interval for Major Equipment and Services		
	Reliability			
	1	HVAC System		
2.4	2	Water Supply & Drainage		
	3	Electrical Equipment		
	4	Support Method of Machines & Ducts		
	5	Communications & IT Equipment		

CASBEE			LEED	
	Categories & Contents		Categories	Contents
3.1	Spatial Margin			
	1	Allowance for Floor-to-floor Height		
	2	Adaptability of Floor Layout		
3.2	Floor Load Margin			
	Adaptability of Facilities			
	1	Ease of Air Conditioning Duct Renewal		
3.3	2	Ease of Water Supply and Drain Pipe Renewal		
	3	Ease of Electrical Wiring Renewal		
	4	Ease of Communications Cable Renewal		
	5	Ease of Equipment Renewal		
	6	Provision of Backup Space		
Q3 Outdoor Environment on Site				
1	Preservation & Creation of Biotope		LT	Sensitive Land Protection
			SS	Heat Island Reduction
2	Townscape & Landscape			
3.1	Attention to Local Charcter & Improvement of Comfort		SS	Open Space
3.2	Improvement of the Thermal Environment on Site		SS	Heat Island Reduction
LR1 Energy				
1	Building Thermal Load		EA	Optimize Energy Performance
2	Natural Energy Utilization		EA	Renewable Energy Production
3	Efficiency in Building Service System		EA	Optimize Energy Performance
4.1	Monitoring		EA	Advanced Energy Metering
4.2	Operation & Management System			

Table 3.6 (continued)   *The similarity of CASBEE and LEED*

CASBEE		LEED	
Categories& Contents		Categories	Contents
LR2 Resources & Materials			
1.1	Water Saving	WE	Indoor Water Use Reduction
1.2	Rainwater & Gray Water		
	1 Rainwater Use System	WE	Outdoor Water Use Reduction
	2 Gray Water Reuse System	WE	Indoor Water Use Reduction
2.1	Reducing Usage of Materials	MR	Building Life-Cycle Impact Reduction
2.2	Cotinuing Use of Existing Building Skeleton etc	MR	Building Life-Cycle Impact Reduction
2.3	Use of Recycled Materials as Structural Frame Materials	MR	Building Life-Cycle Impact Reduction
2.4	Use of Recycled Materials as Non-structural Materials	MR	Building Life-Cycle Impact Reduction
2.5	Timber from Sustainable Forestry	MR	Building Product Disclosure and Optimization - Sourcing of Raw Materials
2.6	Reusability of Components and Materials		
3.1	Use of Materials without Harmful Substances	EQ	Low-Emitted Materials
3.2	Avoidance of CFCs and Halons		
	1 Fire Retardant	MR	Building Product Disclosure and Optimization —Environmental Product Declarations
	2 Insulation Materials	MR	Building Product Disclosure and Optimization —Environmental Product Declarations
	3 Refrigerants	EA	Enhanced Refrigerant Management

CASBEE		LEED	
Categories & Contents		Categories	Contents
LR3 Off-site Environment			
1	Consideration of Global Warming	MR	Building Life-Cycle Impact Reduction
2.1	Air Pollution	MR	Building Product Disclosure and Optimization —Environmental Product Declarations
2.2	Heat Island Effect	SS	Heat Island Reduction
	Load on Local Infrastructure		
	1 Reduction of Rainwater Discharge Loads	SS	Rainwater Management
2.3	2 Sewage Load Suppression	LT	Surrounding Density and Diverse Uses / Access to Quality Transit / Bicycle Facilities / Green Vehicles
	3 Traffic Load Control		
	4 Waste Treatment Loads	MR	Storage and Collection of Recyclables
3.1	Noise, Vibration & Odor		
	1 Noise		
	2 Vibration		
	3 Odor		
3.2	Wind Damage & Sunlight Obstruction		
	1 Restriction of Wind Damage		
	3 Restriction of Sunlight Obstruction		
3.3	Light Pollution		
	1 Outdoor Illumination and Light that Spills from Interiors	SS	Light Pollution Reduction
	2 Measures for Reflected Solar Glare from Building Walls		
	Total Contents Number		Un-Listed Contents Number
	91		44
	Similarity		51.65%

Note: LEED Categories: LT: Location and Transportation; SS: Sustainable Sites; WE: Water Efficiency; EA: Energy and Atmosphere; MR: Material and Resources; EQ: Indoor Environmental Quality; IN: Innovation.

Table 3.7   The similarity of Green Star and LEED

Green Star — Categories and Contents	Max Points	Points		LEED — Categories and Contents
Management				
Green Star Accredited Professional				
Accredited Professional	1	1	IN	LEED Accredited Professional
Commissioning and Tuning				
Services and Maintainability Review		1		Prerequisite Fundamental Commissioning and Verification
Building Commissioning	4	1	EA	Enhanced Commissioning
				Fundamental Commissioning and Verification
Building Systems Tuning		1	EA	Enhanced Commissioning
				Fundamental Commissioning
Independent Commissioning Agent		1	EA	Fundamental Commissioning and Verification
Adaptation and Resilience				
Implementation of a Climate Adaptation Plan	2	2		
Building Information				
Building Information	1	1	EA	Fundamental Commissioning and Verification
Commitment to Performance				
Environmental Building Performance	2	1		
End of Life Waste Performance		1		
Metering and Monitoring				
Monitoring Systems	1	1	EA	Advanced Energy Metering
Responsible Construction Practices				
Formalised Environmental Management System	2	1		
High Quality Staff Support		1		
Operational Waste				
Performance Pathway—Specialist Plan	1 A	1		
Prescriptive Pathway—Facilities	B	1	MR	Storage and Collection of Recyclables
				Construction and Demolition Waste Management Planning

Green Star			LEED	
Categories and Contents	Max Points	Points		Categories and Contents
Indoor Environment Quality				
Indoor Air Quality				
Ventilation System Attributes	4	1	EQ	Minimum Indoor Air Quality Performance
Provision of Outdoor Air		2	EQ	Enhanced Indoor Air Quality Strategies
Exhaust or Elimination of Pollutants		1	EQ	Enhanced Indoor Air Quality Strategies
Acoustic Comfort				
Internal Noise Levels	3	1	EQ	Acoustic Performance
Reverberation		1	EQ	Acoustic Performance
Acoustic Separation		1	EQ	Acoustic Performance
Lighting Comfort				
General Illuminance and Glare Reduction	3	1	EQ	Interior Lighting
Surface Illuminance		1		
Localised Lighting Control		1	EQ	Interior Lighting
Visual Comfort				
Daylight	3	2	EQ	Daylight
Views		1	EQ	Quality Views
Indoor Pollutants				
Paints, Adhesives, Sealants and Carpets	2	1	EQ	Low-Emitting Materials
Engineered Wood Products		1		
Thermal Comfort				
Thermal Comfort	2	1	EQ	Thermal Comfort
Advanced Thermal Comfort		1	EQ	Thermal Comfort

Table 3.7 (continued)   The similarity of Green Star and LEED

Green Star — Categories and Contents		Max Points	Points	LEED — Points	LEED — Categories and Contents
Energy					
Greenhouse Gas Emissions					
Building Envelope					
Glazing			1		
Lighting	A	20	1	EQ	Interior Lighting
Ventilation and Air-conditioning			1		
Domestic Hot Water Systems					
Accredited GreenPower	D		5	EA	Green Power and Carbon Offsets
NABERS Energy Commitment			20	EA	Optimize Energy Performance
Comparison to a Reference Building Pathway	E		20		
Peak Electricity Demand Reduction					
Prescriptive Pathway	A	2	1		
- On-site Energy Generation					
Performance Pathway	B		2		
- Reference Building					
Transport					
Sustainable Transport					
Performance Pathway	A	10	10	LT	Aaccess to Quality Transit
				LT	Surrounding Density and Diverse Uses
Access by Public Transport			3	LT	Aaccess to Quality Transit
Reduced Car Parking Provision	B		1	LT	Reduced Parking Footprint
Low Emission Vehicle Infrastructure			1	LT	Green Vehicles
Active Transport Facilities			1	LT	Bicycle Facilities
Walkable Neighbourhoods			1	LT	Surrounding Density and Diverse Uses
Water					
Potable Water					
Potable Water – Performance Pathway	A	12	12	WE	Outdoor Water Use Reduction
Sanitary Fixture Efficiency			1	WE	Indoor Water Use Reduction
Rainwater Reuse			1	WE	Indoor Water Use Reduction
Heat Rejection	B		2	WE	Outdoor Water Use Reduction
Landscape Irrigation			1	WE	Outdoor Water Use Reduction
Fire System Test Water			1		

Green Star — Categories and Contents	Max Points	Points	LEED	LEED — Categories and Contents
Materials				
Life Cycle Impacts				
Comparative Life Cycle Assessment	7	A 6	MR	Building Life-Cycle Impact Reduction
Additional Life Cycle Impact Reporting		4	MR	Building Life-Cycle Impact Reduction
Concrete		3		
Steel		1		
Building Reuse		B 4	MR	Building Life-Cycle Impact Reduction
Structural Timber		3		
Responsible Building Materials				
Structural and Reinforcing Steel	3	1		
Timber Products		1	MR	Building Product Disclosure and Optimization-Sourcing of
Permanent Formwork, Pipes, Flooring, Blinds, and Cables		1		
Sustainable Products				
Product Transparency and Sustainability	3	3	MR	Building Life-Cycle Impact Reduction / Building Product Disclosure and Optimization—Environmental Product Declarations
Construction and Demolition Waste				
Fixed Benchmark	1	A 1	MR	Construction and Demolition Waste Management
Percentage Benchmark		B 1	MR	Construction and Demolition Waste Management
Land Use & Ecology				
Ecological Value				
Ecological Value	3	3		
Sustainable Sites				
Reuse of Land	2	1	LT	High-Priority Site
Contamination and Hazardous Materials		1	LT	High-Priority Site
Heat Island Effect				
Heat Island Effect Reduction	1	1	SS	Open Space / Heat Island Reduction

Table 3.7 (continued)　　　*The similarity of Green Star and LEED*

Green Star			LEED			
Categories and Contents	Max Points	Points		Categories and Contents	Total Contents Number Un-Listed Point Max	Total Contents Number (Un-Listed Point Minimum)
Emissions						
Stormwater						
Stormwater Peak Discharge	2	1	SS	Rainwater Management		
Stormwater Pollution Targets		1				
Light Pollution						
Light Pollution to Night Sky	1	1	SS	Light Pollution Reduction		
Microbial Control						
Legionella Impacts from Cooling Systems	1	1				
Refrigerant Impacts						
Refrigerants Impacts	1	1	EA	Enhanced Refrigerant Management		
Un-Listed Points Minimum	Listed Points	Un Listed Points Maximum			Un-Listed Contents (Un-Listed Point Maximum)	Un-Listed Contents (Un-Listed Point Minimum)
19	100	48			48	59
81.00%	Similarity	52.00%			24	14
					50.00%	76.27%

Note: LEED Categories: IP: Integrative Process; LT: Location and Transportation; SS: Sustainable Sites; WE: Water Efficiency; EA: Energy and Atmosphere; MR: Material and Resources; EQ: Indoor Environmental Quality; IN: Innovation.

construction companies and professionals in the industry of the country to gain the skills and experiences of two considerably different rating systems. When the governments or other entities develop local rating systems, it is critically important to assess the trade-offs between the benefit and costs of owning local rating systems and to consider harmonization of such local rating systems with a global rating systems to mitigate the inevitable costs.

Table 3.8   *Similarity with LEED and association with the number of LEED buildings*

	Similarity with LEED	Association and significance with the number of LEED buildings
CASBEE (Japan)	51.7%: Item	Significant (Negative)
Green Star (Australia)	50–76.3%: Item 52.0–81.0%: Score	Significant (Negative)
BREEAM (UK and others)	90.1%: Item 90.9%: Score	Not significant

3.4   CONCLUSION

Voluntary green building rating systems are one of the most important policy tools to reduce GHG emission from the construction sector and other sustainable development goals globally. In this chapter, we have conducted a quantitative and qualitative analysis on how country-specific and global green building rating systems interact and presented policy implications for decision makers to design country- and context-specific green building rating systems. Country- and context-specific green building rating systems are strongly needed and are expected to grow, and this study indicates such systems should be compatible and harmonized with global green building rating system such as LEED to keep the benefit of introducing local systems while mitigating its costs.

REFERENCES

Accame, F., Cesare, J., Chen, Y., Walsh, E., and Wu, Q. (2012). Green buildings in the US and China: Bridging the energy performance gap. Bren School of Environmental Science & Management Work Project Final Report.

Alyami, S.H., Rwzgui, Y., and Kwan, A. (2015). The development of sustainable assessment method for Saudi Arabia built environment: Weighting system. *Sustainability Science*, 10(1), 167–78, doi: 10.1007/s11625-014-0252-x.

Asensio, O.I., and Delmas, M.A. (2017). The effectiveness of US energy efficiency building labels. *Nature Energy*, 2(4), 17033.

BREEAM website, https://www.breeam.com/ (last accessed January 2019).

CASBEE website, IBEC, http://www.ibec.or.jp/CASBEE/ (last accessed January 2019).

Darko, A., Chan, A.P., Huo, X., and Owusu-Manu, D.G. (2019). A scientometric analysis and visualization of global green building research. *Building and Environment*, 149, 501–11, doi: 10.1016/j.buildenv.2018.12.059.

Doan, D.T., Ghaffarianhoseini, A., Naismith, N., Zhang, T., Ghaffarianhoseini, A., and Tookey, J. (2017). A critical comparison of green building rating systems. *Building and Environment*, 123, 243–60, doi: 10.1016/j.buildenv.2017.07.007.

Green Star website, Green Building Council Australia, https://new.gbca.org.au/green-star/rating-system/ (last accessed January 2019).

Hoffert, M.I., Caldeira, K., Benford, G. et al. (2002). Advanced technology paths to global climate stability: Energy for a greenhouse planet. *Science*, 298(5595), 981–7, doi: 10.1126/science.1072357.

LEED website, US Green Building Council (USGBC), https://new.usgbc.org/leed (last accessed November 2018).

Lucon, O., Ürge-Vorsatz, D., Zain Ahmed, A. et al. (2014). Buildings. In: *Climate Change 2014: Mitigation of Climate Change. Contribution of Working Group III to the Fifth Assessment Report of the Intergovernmental Panel on Climate Change.* Cambridge and New York: Cambridge University Press. Retrieved from https://www.ipcc.ch/pdf/assessment-report/ar5/wg3/ipcc_wg3_ar5_chapter9.pdf (last accessed January 2019).

Mattoni, B., Guattari, C., Evangelisti, L., Bisegna, F., Gori, P., and Asdrubali, F. (2018). Critical review and methodological approach to evaluate the differences among international green building rating tools. *Renewable and Sustainable Energy Reviews*, 82, 950–60, doi: 10.1016/j.rser.2017.09.105.

Open Doors (2018). International students by place of origin, 2016/17, 2017/18. Retrieved from https://www.iie.org/Research-and-Insights/Open-Doors (last accessed November 2018).

World Bank Climate Change Knowledge Portal (2011). Historical data. Retrieved from https://datacatalog.worldbank.org/dataset/climate-change-knowledge-portal-historical-data (last accessed November 2018).

World Green Building Council, List of green building rating tools. Retrieved from https://www. worldgbc.org/rating-tools (last accessed November 2018).

Zou, Y., Zhao, W., and Zhong, R. (2017). The spatial distribution of green buildings in China: Regional imbalance, economic fundamentals, and policy incentives. *Applied Geography*, 88, 38–47.

4. Diffusion mechanisms for regulating fishery products: the cases of Tanzania, Madagascar, and Mauritius

Akiko Yanai

4.1   INTRODUCTION

The protection of public health by ensuring food safety and quality has always been a fundamental function of states. Since food safety hazards can occur at any stage of the food chain, each government necessarily establishes its own food safety regulations to control the entire food chain and to monitor the whole delivery process. Fishery products are one kind of food that requires strict measures to maintain food safety due to their tendency to be easily perishable and contaminated. In order to deliver marine products to consumers safely and hygienically, governments, especially those in developed countries, have developed stringent regulatory systems ensuring the safety and quality of fishery products.

With the globalization of food systems, however, these kinds of regulations and standards can hinder the trade of food, especially when developing countries export to developed markets. Some studies have shown that the main restrictions for developing countries to access the markets of developed countries are currently not tariff but non-tariff barriers (NTBs), particularly product and food safety regulations (Czubala et al., 2009; Henson et al., 2000: 1159; Kareem, 2016: 84). The issue of food safety has become a global concern, "not only for its continuing importance to public health, but also because of its impact on international trade" (Barendsz, 1998: 163). In overcoming these restrictions, countries tend toward reducing NTBs by harmonizing the legal system or mutual recognition. In addition to these methods, diffusion of the policy or the regulation of a certain country to another country is one of the paths to diminish NTBs.

For fishery products, compliance with the food safety regulations of the export destination country has been a necessary condition in accessing its markets. As a result, the legal systems of developing countries are often influenced by the regulations of developed countries. As discussed in the introductory chapter of this volume, the diffusion that occurs with respect to food safety regulations on fishery products involves competition and coercion motivations. However, it is not clear what the mechanism of policy diffusion is between the leader (developed) countries and follower (developing) countries. Moreover, even if policy diffusion results from the same motivation, such as the desire to gain or continue to access export markets, the extent and speed of modification can differ depending on the country. Therefore, it is necessary to pay attention to the process in which the regulations of the importing country are become rules of the exporting country in order to examine this diffusion mechanism in depth. It is also necessary to conduct a comparative study of several developing countries.

The issue of NTBs is vital to African exports. Therefore, the development of domestic laws in three jurisdictions—Tanzania, Madagascar, and Mauritius—are examined in this chapter. All three countries regard fishing as an important industry and actively promote the export of their fish products, mainly to the European Union (EU).

To consider the mechanisms of policy diffusion of fishery regulations in developing countries, it is necessary to examine whether national regulations are influenced by other legal frameworks and whether, as a result, there are differences in the national regulations of each developing country. In answering these inquiries, the second section explores various legal frameworks regarding fishery products in terms of food safety, with a special focus on the international regulations and the EU regulations, which is the largest export market for the selected three African countries (Section 4.2). To analyze the diffusion mechanism of EU policy to these developing countries, the third section examines the actions of both sides: the EU's audit system as importers and the responses to the EU's audits by these three African countries as exporters (Section 4.3). The last section considers the factors affecting the differences in the diffusion mechanisms of each of the three countries (Section 4.4).

4.2   LEGAL FRAMEWORKS CONCERNING THE FOOD SAFETY OF FISHERY PRODUCTS

The state has a sovereign right for ensuring food safety in its jurisdiction. Thus, it has created efficient food safety systems, including implementing sanitary and phytosanitary (SPS) measures. However, since food chains exist across national borders because of globalization, the legal system on food safety of each country becomes influenced by various other regulatory measures. Especially when exporting foods overseas, managing hygiene in accordance with international standards as well as complying with the regulations of importing countries is required. Therefore, when developing countries develop food safety regulations for marine products, they ought to take into account at least two regulatory frameworks: international standards and the requirements of importing countries.

4.2.1 International Frameworks

Legislation governing food safety varies widely from country to country. The differences between national food regulations often make it difficult to trade food across borders (FAO and WTO, 2017: 3). Conventionally, therefore, SPS measures have been regarded as trade impediments, especially for developing countries.[1] For eliminating obstacles to trade, international legal frameworks regarding food safety have been developed by harmonizing each national standard or by concluding new international agreements. Under such international agreements, SPS compliance can be taken to include national obligations (Day et al., 2012: 19).

4.2.1.1 Codex standards

Since its inception in 1963, Codex Alimentarius (CODEX) has attempted to harmonize food and commodity standards and has provided guidelines, recommendations, and codes of practice designed to protect the health of consumers and ensure free, safe, and fair trade practices. There are three kinds of CODEX standards: (i) food standards for deciding the criteria; (ii) recommendations, mainly for sanitary issues; and (iii) guidelines, for example, how to implement Hazard Analysis and Critical Control Point (HACCP). These CODEX materials serve as a minimum benchmark for countries to establish national food safety legislation. For those countries that have a structured food regulatory system, the CODEX provisions are often considered the relevant reference regulations when the national food law does not have any specific provisions. For those countries with underdeveloped national laws, the CODEX standards are generally referred to or may even be directly adopted into their food safety system.[2] A member state designates a national CODEX contact point (NCCP) that coordinates all relevant CODEX activities within the country and establishes a national CODEX committee (NCC) to supplement the work of the NCCP (WHO, 2012: 1). One of their main activities is to adopt CODEX standards as national standards (Ayalew et al., 2013: 436).

4.2.1.2 HACCP

HACCP is a hygiene management system that ensures food safety by identifying and controlling hazards at specific points in the processing chain, from raw material production to the consumption of the final product. The idea of HACCP was created by the American Apollo program in order to ensure the safety of space food, but after that, it was adapted to various foods[3] and spread throughout the world. CODEX provided HACCP guidelines in 1993, recognizing it as the general principles of food hygiene; many developed countries have since made HACCP mandatory. HACCP is now an international standard for maintaining food safety, and developing countries have also adopted HACCP. However, they adopted it primarily because their major destination areas for export, like the EU and the United States (US), require food to be processed in accordance with HACCP as an import condition (Donovan et al., 2001: 164). In other words, developing countries did not necessarily adopt HACCP into their own food safety systems because they regard HACCP as an international standard with which to comply.

4.2.1.3   The WTO Agreement on SPS Measures (the SPS Agreement)

The SPS Agreement came into effect on January 1, 1995 with the establishment of the World Trade Organization (WTO). The SPS Agreement provides the basic rules related to safety measures for internationally traded foods. It stipulates that SPS measures should be applied only to the extent necessary to protect human, animal, or plant life and should not be applied in such a manner as to constitute disguised restrictions on international trade (Article 2). In order to harmonize SPS measures on as wide a basis as possible, the SPS Agreement also encourages member countries to base their SPS measures on international standards, guidelines, or recommendations, where they exist (Article 3). For food safety, the SPS Agreement specifies the CODEX standards as these "international standards, guidelines, or recommendations" (Annex A.3). This is because the WTO in itself is not a standard setting but a standard ruling organization (Will, 2012: 23).

These international legal frameworks have certainly influenced the development of food safety regulations in developing countries. Under the WTO rules, SPS measures for imported foods should be based on the CODEX standards. Even though the WTO member countries do not necessarily have to comply with the CODEX standards because of their voluntary nature, the CODEX standards are currently regarded as the international principle of food trade, which each country should take into consideration when setting their food safety standards. Also, HAACP is now well established as a process standard adopted by many countries. Given the increasing reliance on process standards, more responsibility is placed on domestic regulations in exporting countries than in border inspections in importing countries (Orden and Roberts, 2007: 115).

4.2.2   EU's Food Safety Requirements on Fishery Products

Developed countries often impose more stringent requirements than the international standards for reducing food safety risks. Such domestic regulations apply to all foods distributed in the country, no matter whether domestically produced or imported. Considering that developing countries often suffer from "a lack of administrative, technical and scientific capacities" (Murina and Nicita, 2014: 2) such as inadequate production facilities, it is particularly difficult for them to satisfy the requirements of developed countries (Wahidin and Purnhagen, 2018: 17).

As the largest importer of fishery products in the world, while at the same time having the most stringent food safety standards, the EU's food safety regulations function as the de facto standards for exporters. Thus, developing countries consider EU regulations more crucial than international standards such as CODEX when developing their own SPS-related legislation.[4] The EU food safety regulations distinguish between animal-derived foods and non-animal-derived foods and impose stricter restrictions on the former. These strict regulations also apply to imported fishery products.

The current system of the EU's food safety legislation is based on the General Food Law Regulation (178/2002), which lays down general principles, requirements, and procedures in matters of food safety, covering all stages of food and feed production and distribution. One of the characteristics of the law is to impose traceability requirements throughout the food chain.

In order to conform to the general principles specified by the General Food Law Regulation, the EU made fundamental amendments to food-related laws and regulations in 2004. Specifically, the EU updated its food hygiene regulations and integrated them as the "Hygiene Package," which came into force in January 2006. This set of regulations consists of three regulations: the General Good Sanitation Regulation (852/2004), which lays down the general hygiene requirements for all of the food business operators; the Animal Origin Foods Regulation (853/2004), which lays down additional specific requirements for food businesses dealing with foods of animal origin, including fishery products; and the Origin Food Special Public Control Regulation (854/2004), which lays down the official controls for foods of animal origin. These new regulations focus on the need to protect public health in an effective way. A key aspect of the new legislation is that all food and feed business operators, from producers and processors to retailers and caterers, will have the principal responsibility for ensuring that food placed on the EU market meets the required food safety standards. The new regulations apply at every stage in the food chain, regardless of whether business operators are in the EU or outside of the EU.[5] In addition, fishery products need to comply with regulations on heavy metals and persistent organic pollutants (POPs),[6] the rules on food additives,[7] and food packaging regulations.[8]

Countries exporting fishery products to the EU have to be accredited by the EU as an eligible country for exporting fishery products as a pre-requisite.[9] The criteria of this eligibility are to have a competent authority, to fulfil the relevant EU food safety requirements, and to control approved vessels and establishments.

4.3   THE DIFFUSION PROCESS FOR EU REGULATIONS

As the EU generally imposes higher levels of health protection, the EU regulations on food safety exceed those that are effective in developing countries. The introduction of the new hygiene standards in 2004 is a typical example of what happened in developing countries afterward. With the implementation of this hygiene package, countries outside of the EU had to adopt health and sanitary regulations at least equivalent to the ones required within the EU. Competent authorities of exporting countries also had to implement effective inspection and guarantee the newly required level of food safety and quality by issuing credible health certificates on fishery products that are destined for the EU.[10] In terms of the fishery industry, food business operators needed to implement specific HACCP-based sanitary practices in their work areas such as catching, handling, processing, and packaging fishery products (Neeliah et al., 2011: 61).

4.3.1   EU's Audit System

Aiming to ensure that the EU legislation on food safety is properly implemented and enforced in the countries outside of the EU, the EU carries out audits, inspections, and related non-audit activities. The European Commission's Food and Veterinary Office (FVO) conducts regular inspection to verify whether the competent authorities have an effective control system for foods and assess compliance with the EU regulatory requirements. Whereas support projects have been effective in improving the level of food safety in developing countries in terms of production capacity and fishery technology, audits are very important in terms of rule enforcement. After the introduction of the new hygiene regulations, the EU conducted audits for Tanzania, Madagascar, and Mauritius, which export fishery products to the EU market (Table 4.1).

During the audit carried out in September 2006 in Tanzania, for example, the audit mission team paid particular attention to the level of equivalency of relevant Tanzanian legislation and to the ability of the competent authorities to deliver the required standards of these new EU rules in regard to products destined for EU export. The team had meetings with related ministries and agencies in Tanzania, such as the Fisheries Division of the Ministry of Natural Resources and Tourism and the Central Competent Authority. It also visited district fisheries offices, laboratories, fishing vessels, freezer vessels, fishery products processing establishments, and so on.

Table 4.1   List of EU's audits to Tanzania, Madagascar, and Mauritius

Tanzania	
August 1999	Controls on pesticide residues in fish coming from Lake Victoria
October 2000	Fishery products (pesticides)
September–October 2006	Fishery products
June 2011	Fishery products
September 2017	Export controls—plants and plant products
Madagascar	
February–March 2005	Fishery products
March 2007	Fishery and aquaculture products
June 2012	Fishery products
Mauritius	
August 1998	Fishery products
January 2006	Fishery products
February 2008	Fishery products
March–April 2009	Animal health—equidae for export to EU
November 2009	Fishery products
January 2014	Fishery products

Source: The EU's website on audit reports.[11]

After the audit, the mission team found that the Tanzanian current regulation, the Fisheries Regulations 2005, included provisions that were considered at least equivalent to EU requirements. However, the FVO noted discrepancies with EU rules, such as:

• Water temperature in taps: the Fisheries Regulations 2005 does not presently include provisions for the presence of hot and cold running water for wash-hand basins (EU Regulation No. 852/2004, Annex II, Chapter I, p. 4);
• The Fisheries Regulations 2005 does not include the species sensitive for histamine formation mentioned in the EU legislation (FVO, 2006b: 5).

As a result, the FVO recommended to the Competent Authority of Tanzania regarding legislation as below (FVO, 2006b: 16):

> Recommendations to the Competent Authority of Tanzania
> The Central Competent Authority were asked to provide Commission services with a detailed action plan, including a timetable for its completion within 25 working days of receipt of the report, in order to address the following recommendations for fishery products intended for export to the EU:
>
> 5.1. Legislation
> With regard to controlling and certifying fishery products intended for export to the EU, the competent Authority should update the current standards applicable to export to the EU in order to ensure equivalence with Community standards on contaminants (Regulation (EC) No 466/2001), additives (Directive 95/2/EC), potable water (Directive 98/83/EC), hygiene (Regulations (EC) No 852/2004 and 853/2004), and official controls (Regulations (EC) No 854/2004 and 882/2004).

For the 2005 audit in Madagascar, the mission team recommended to the Malagasy authorities to "amend or supplement existing legislation so that it contains identical or equivalent guarantees to those provided in Community legislation" (FVO, 2005: 2). This recommendation applied to various issues, such as standards for water potability, as well as the monitoring of these standards, and maximum levels of certain contaminants in fishery products. The audit team also requested that:

> [t]he Malagasy competent authority should be given appropriate financing and equipment, and qualified staff who have undergone specific training in fishery and aquaculture products in order to be able to perform effective and uniform checks on the application of the legislation in force and carry out the official checks required under Community legislation (FVO, 2005: 2).

During the 2006 Mauritius audit, the FVO found that "a number of texts applicable to the national market (e.g. water, contaminants)—that could be also used in the context of the exports to the EU—are not in line with all the Community requirements" (FVO, 2006a: 5). The FVO recommended in its inspection report to the Mauritian government that "[t]he CA [competent authority] should respect Community requirements when controlling and certifying fishery products exported to the EU as no Mauritian specific national legislation equivalent to the relevant Community requirements exists" (FVO, 2006a: 13). Two years after the audit, the follow-up inspection took place in order to "verify the extent to which the guarantees and the corrective actions submitted to the Commission services in response to the recommendations of a previous FVO mission report ... have been implemented, enforced and controlled" (FVO, 2008: 1).

4.3.2   The Response from the African Countries

4.3.2.1   Tanzania

4.3.2.1.1   General legal framework on fisheries
The existing legal and regulatory framework of the fisheries sector in Tanzania depends on the National Fisheries Sector Policy and Strategy Statements (1997), which were established to promote the fishery industry, utilize sustainable resources, secure food, create employment, and export industries. To implement the 1997 fishery policy, several legal provisions exist in different legal and regulatory frameworks. Among them, the Fisheries Act, 2003[12] is the main legal text for the governance of fisheries, and the Fisheries Regulations, 2009, is the principal law for implementation; the 2009 Regulations stipulate detailed provisions, such as fishery licenses, a fishing vessel registration system, as well as a resource management system. The 2009 Regulations also regulate trade, hygiene, and HACCP. These rules were developed in line with the export standard requirement of the EU (Lee and Namisi, 2016: 20).

For Tanzania, fishery products are relatively new export commodities. Tanzania actively started exporting fishery products in the mid-1990s. Before exporting fishery products, Tanzania had only simple food safety standards regarding fishery products. After independence in 1951, the development of food legislation inevitably was of low priority because the main focus was on efforts to increase production of export crops and to prevent malnutrition (Jukes, 1988: 295). The Food and Drugs (Standards of Quality) Regulations, which were amended in 1971, set some food hygiene standards for consumer protection; they were based on old British legislation, and they were far from modernized and were not comprehensive food safety regulations.

However, the situation has drastically changed since 1997 when two food safety crises occurred in fish caught on Lake Victoria. The first was contamination with *Salmonella* and the other was an outbreak of cholera in East Africa (Day et al., 2012: 21–2). Because of the cholera epidemic, the EU imposed a ban on all fish exports from the lake to the EU market. Tanzania, along with Kenya and Uganda, who were also engaged in fishing activity on Lake Victoria, embarked on a massive hygiene program in fish handling as well as in the processing establishments around the lake. In addition to this export ban, Tanzania received another EU export ban on fishery products due to pesticide use in 1999. Many projects were implemented to improve food safety standards, which mostly included the CODEX codes of hygiene for fishing (Ministry of Industry, Trade and Marketing, United Republic of Tanzania,

2011: 39). It is worth noting that these projects were carried out with strong cooperation from EU countries. This experience has had a significant impact on Tanzania's desire to meet EU regulations. Actually, the Food and Drugs Act has been amended to include requirements such as HACCP as well as pollutant and pest limits, to comply with EU legislation on food safety.

4.3.2.1.2 Attitudes toward the EU's 2004 hygiene package
Responding to the recommendations of the audit report (DG SANCO 8241/2006) carried out in October 2006, the Competent Authority of Tanzania submitted its action plan to the FVO. Regarding amendment of legislation, the competent authority started a process to review the Fisheries Regulations 2005 regarding the points below:

- Limits for heavy metals (i.e. mercury, lead, and cadmium), additives, and potable water parameters have been incorporated; for histamine and sodium, meta-bisulphite analysis has also been incorporated.
- The amended draft for Fisheries Regulations 2005 also provides for analyses of polycyclic aromatic hydrocarbons (PAH) and dioxin in fishery products and potable water.
- Concerning poisonous fish, the Gempilidae family has been included.
- There is also a provision for hot potable water supply in hand wash basins in the fish establishment.
- The Fisheries Regulations 2005 have been amended to provide for proper procedures for the approval of fish establishments as well as for their suspension, closure, and de-listing (CAT, 2006).

The competent authority promised to submit a copy of the reviewed Fisheries Regulations, 2005, to the FVO or the EC by July 2007. However, it took more time to review and amend the regulations, and Tanzania adopted the new EU hygiene package into its legal system in 2009, when the country conducted a large-scale amendment of its fishery regulations.

4.3.2.2 Madagascar

4.3.2.2.1 General legal framework on fisheries
The framework for regulating fishing activities in Madagascar is based on the Fisheries Act (Ordonnance 93-022 du 04 mai 1993 portant réglementation de lapêche et de l'aquaculture) (Humber et al., 2015). This Act supersedes all major international agreements on fisheries (Breuil and Grima, 2014: 27). However, if the obligations imposed by international agreements are renewed, national regulations will need to be adjusted. National regulations are often reviewed and revised if necessary based on the recommendation of

the projects implemented by such donor countries and institutions as the EU.[13] Whereas the Ministry of Agriculture, Livestock, and Fisheries is primarily responsible for implementing government fishery policies, Autorité Sanitaire Halieutique (ASH) focuses on ensuring food safety as the competent authority in Madagascar. The government actively supported seafood exporters by establishing an effective inspection system for fishery products as well as pursuing capacity building for meeting the quality standards of the HACCP.

4.3.2.2.2   Attitudes toward the EU's 2004 hygiene package

Madagascar introduced its general framework of food safety regulations largely based on the international legal frameworks, referring to international standards such as CODEX and HACCP. The country's fishery management policy now complies with international regulations, and the detailed provisions are compliant with EU regulations. As the EU rules changed, the relevant laws of Madagascar were modified accordingly, as there is now even an officer in charge of periodically monitoring changes in the EU legal system.[14] As to the EU hygiene package of 2004, it was implemented into the following Malagasy laws: EU Regulation 852/2004 was put into Arrêté No. 2910/2007; EU Regulation 853/2004 was put into Arrêté No. 2908/2007; and EU Regulation 854/2004 was put into Arrêté No. 2907/2007. These regulations were signed by the minister of agriculture in December 2007, which the EU FVO considered as equivalent to the relevant EU requirements in the audit done in 2007 (FVO, 2007: 5).

4.3.2.3   Mauritius

4.3.2.3.1   General law and policy on fisheries

The government of Mauritius has a national fishery plan that aims to implement (i) sustainable resource use and protection of the marine environment, and (ii) maximize returns from existing fisheries through value addition.[15] Based on the plan, the Ministry of Fisheries prioritizes conservation of the marine environment within the lagoon as well as the promotion of sustainable micro fisheries. The Fisheries and Marine Resources Act 1998 (FMRA) provides the principles for fisheries and marine living resources management. It has provisions regarding marine protected areas, prohibition of fishing, prohibition of the sale of toxic fish and fish products, and licensing of local and foreign boats and vessels. As to the issue of food safety, while the basic law is the Food Act 1998, domestic hygiene regulations are primarily based on CODEX (Neeliah et al., 2011: 62). Unique to Mauritius is the fact that it has a competent authority that specializes in fishery products. The Competent Authority Seafood is a public agency under the Ministry of Blue Economy, Marine Resources, Fisheries and Shipping and is responsible for the verification and certification of fish and fish products for export. It is noteworthy that the Competent Authority Seafood itself considers its primary role as inspecting export seafood destined to the EU.

4.3.2.3.2 *Attitudes toward the EU's 2004 hygiene package*
Reacting to the recommendations of the FVO audit in 2006, Mauritius promptly—specifically only one month after the audit—promulgated the Fisheries and Marine Resources (Export of Fish and Fish Products) Regulations (No. 2) 2006 (Government Notice No. 27 of 2006).[16] The regulation stipulates that "No person shall export from Mauritius any fish or fishery products unless … (b) he complies with the standards applicable in the importing country" (Article 5). Thus, EU standards are directly and automatically applicable in the case of export to any EU Member State (FVO, 2008: 4). The Mauritius government has taken further steps and carried out regulatory reform in 2007 to be in line with EU requirements for fish exports (Neeliah et al., 2011: 63). Moreover, Mauritius strengthened the institutions to implement SPS measures that the EU has required in its audit report. For example, the Fisheries and Marine Resources (Export of Fish and Fish Products) Regulations (No. 2) 2006 (Government Notice No. 148 of 2006) empowered the Division of Veterinary Services as a competent authority for verification and certification of fish and fish products intended for export (FVO, 2008: 4). Also, in order to enhance the ability of the inspection capacity, a consultant was appointed to review the activities of the competent authority (Neeliah et al., 2013: 59).

4.3.2.4 Sub-conclusion
Since the EU requires that all fishery products distributed in its market meet EU standards, the EU regulations on food safety have a major impact on the African fishing sector. To maintain access to this important export market, all the governments of Tanzania, Madagascar, and Mauritius passed a series of laws that made their own food safety standards equivalent to the ones of the EU. In this sense, as stated in the introduction of this book, the motivation for these three African countries to adopt the EU regulations was to maintain access to export markets. At the same time, the EU conducts periodic and systematic audits to ensure and maintain the food safety standards of exporting countries. It assesses whether each government is capable of implementing the required standards on fishery products exported to the EU. In the audit recommendations, the EU states clearly what actions these African countries should take and the deadline for achieving them. The EU's interactive approach toward exporting countries is also a major factor facilitating diffusion of these EU regulations to Tanzania, Madagascar, and Mauritius.

4.4 FACTORS INFLUENCING THE RAPIDITY OF DIFFUSION

In terms of food safety standards on fishery products, the three African countries under study accepted the new EU regulations by amending their own respective national legal framework. Because the EU is such a large seafood export market for each country, market access needs to be maintained. However, the speed in which each country responded to the new EU regulations differed. For example, the EU introduced its higher standards in 2004, and in response, Mauritius and Madagascar implemented legal amendments in 2007, and Tanzania implemented its own in 2009. This difference resulted mainly from two factors: market importance and the existence of regional standards.

4.4.1 Market Importance

4.4.1.1 Tanzania
Tanzanian fishing consists of marine and inland water fishery. Over the last decade, Tanzania's fish production has been in the range of 325,000 to 380,000 tons per annum (Ministry of Agriculture, Livestock, and Fisheries, United Republic of Tanzania, 2016: 4). About 85% of the country's total production is from inland fisheries, and 14% is from marine fisheries.[17] The aquaculture industry has been gradually developing since the 1990s, but the share of the total catch is as low as 1%. The fishing sector accounted for 1.4% of the gross domestic product (GDP) in 2015.

The export value of fishery products was 193 million US dollars in 2017, which accounted for about 10% of the total catch and 5% of the total commodity exports. In Tanzania, the Nile perch processing industry, which began in the early 1990s, has boosted the exports of fishery products dramatically.[18] The main export partners are EU member countries, China, and the Middle East, particularly the United Arab Emirates and Israel. Tanzania also exports to neighboring countries: the Democratic Republic of Congo, Kenya, Uganda, Malawi, and Rwanda (Table 4.2).

Tanzania recognizes that fish is an important source of protein for its people. Only 10% of the total catch is exported, and the rest is for domestic markets. Therefore, Tanzania is not desperate to maintain food safety standards that are equivalent to those of the EU.

Table 4.2   Tanzania's key indicators of its fishery sector

Production (in 2015)	381 970 t
Wild catch	371 228 t
Aquaculture	10 742 t
Export (in 2017)	192 766 (1000 US$)
Share of total export	4.2%
Destination:	
EU	52.8%
Netherlands	15.6%
Portugal	7.9%
Spain	7.4%
Italy	6.6%
Belgium	5.2%
Others	10.0%
China (incl. Hong Kong)	21.5%
United Arab Emirates	7.2%
Israel	5.1%
Vietnam	2.4%
Japan	2.3%
EAC (Uganda, Kenya, Burundi, and Rwanda)	2.9%
Others	5.8%

Source: FAO annual fisheries statistics (2015), UN Comtrade.

4.4.1.2   Madagascar

Because it is a large island in the Indian Ocean, Madagascar has a long coastline and a huge exclusive economic zone (EEZ). In inland areas, there are rivers, marshes, and wetlands, which form diverse ecosystems. Utilizing such a naturally rich environment, the fisheries sector in Madagascar currently produces an estimated 120,000 tons per year, and marine fisheries dominate the fisheries sector with 70% of total production.[19] The export value of fishery products was 140 million US dollars in 2017, which accounts for about 20% of the total catch and 5% of the total commodity exports. The main export partners are the EU (76.2%), especially France (70.1%), and China (16.6%) (Table 4.3).

Table 4.3   *Madagascar's key indicators of its fishery sector*

Production (in 2015)	113 954 t
Wild catch	91 260 t
Aquaculture	22 694 t
Export (in 2017)	138 045 (1000 US$)
Share of total export	4.9%
Destination:	
EU	76.2%
France	70.1%
Spain	3.8%
Portugal	2.1%
Others	0.2%
China (incl. Hong Kong)	16.6%
Japan	2.6%
Mauritius	2.5%
Others	2.1%

Source: FAO annual fisheries statistics (2015), UN Comtrade.

4.4.1.3 Mauritius

As an island nation, Mauritius has rich fishing grounds. Besides cane sugar, which is the major export item, seafood exports are becoming more important. Mauritius's fishery production increased from 7,366 tons in 2010 to 18,062 tons in 2016, and the export of 403 million US dollars in 2017 accounted for 20% of the total commodity exports. Its current export partners include the EU (33.0%), Japan (18.8%), Thailand (11.0%), China (8.7%), and the US (6.8%) (Table 4.4). Even though the share of EU as an exporting market of Mauritius fish products is lower than for Madagascar and Tanzania, the EU market is quite strong for the Mauritius economy, as the share of marine product trade in exports as a whole is large; in 2018, it comprised 22.3%, as compared to 4.2% for Tanzania and 4.9% for Madagascar. This high percentage is because Mauritius has a large canned tuna industry that exports to the EU.

Moreover, with the erosion of the Sugar Protocol, Mauritius cannot rely solely on the export of sugar and now has to exploit alternative export avenues, such as fish and horticultural products, which are considered as high value in export markets (FAO, 2014; MOAIF, 2008). Currently, Mauritius has put in place a policy to replace declining sugar exports with seafood exports. For this reason, the EU market is very important but is threatened by the stringency of the EU's food regulations (Neeliah and Neeliah, 2014). In order to maintain and expand its fish exports, Mauritius has had to respond to these requirements by providing high quality and safe products (Daby, 2003; Neeliah and Neeliah, 2014).

Table 4.4   Mauritius's key indicators of its fishery sector

Production (in 2015)	19 083 t
Wild catch	18 062 t
Aquaculture	1021 t
Export (in 2017)	403 411 (1000 US$)
Share of total export	22.3%
Destination:	
EU	33.0%
Spain	16.2%
France	6.7%
Portugal	4.7%
Italy	2.8%
United Kingdom	2.2%
Others	0.4%
Japan	18.8%
Thailand	11.0%
China (incl. Hong Kong)	9.4%
US	6.8%
Vietnam	4.4%
Singapore	3.8%
New Zealand	1.3%
Others	5.7%

Source: FAO annual fisheries statistics (2015), UN Comtrade.

4.4.1.4 Sub-conclusion

The diffusion of EU regulations on food safety into these African countries strongly depends on the importance of the EU market for the economy of each country. The main destination of fishing exports for the three African countries in this study is the European market, which emphasizes the relevance of adhering to EU requirements to secure and maintain exports. However, this study finds variation in attitudes toward adopting EU regulations. Mauritius, even though its dependency ratio to the EU as an export market is low at 33%, is the most dependent of the three countries on the EU fishery market; hence, it has shown a highly reactive attitude to complying with the new EU SPS measures. Madagascar, the second most dependent country on the EU market, has paid serious attention to the changes in the EU standards and has sought to follow them by amending its relevant laws. However, Tanzania, which exports 50% of its marine products to the EU market, has not shown a prompt response to the EU standard raising. Rather, it seems to be prioritizing conforming to the regional standards, namely, those of the East African Community (EAC), a topic that is explained in the next section.

4.4.2   Existence of Regional Laws

The existence of regional standards is one of the factors explaining differences in diffusion rapidity among the three African countries. Currently, every African country belongs to at least one regional organization, usually several, and each cooperates with one another concerning various policy issues affecting member countries. For the three countries under study, Tanzania belongs to the EAC[20] and the Southern African Development Community (SADC);[21] Both Madagascar and Mauritius are members of the Common Market for Eastern and Southern Africa (COMESA)[22] and the SADC.

Since the 1960s, when many African countries achieved independence, economic integration in Africa has been regarded as an effective and key vehicle for Africa's economic development. Therefore, several regional cohesive economic groups have made efforts toward trade liberalization. As a result, a number of regional economic communities (RECs) have been organized to date, forming customs unions and free trade areas. Each REC has developed its own roadmap for economic integration and is currently implementing programs to form free trade areas, customs unions, or common markets. The degree of progress in economic integration varies among RECs. For example, COMESA and the SADC are in the process of forming a free trade area, while the EAC has already formed a customs union and is in the process of creating a common market.

The standardization authorities of EAC countries have been seeking to promote trade flows to and between EAC countries by eliminating unnecessary barriers to trade. To achieve this objective as well as to protect the health and safety of society and the environment in the region, the EAC member countries have enacted the East African Community Standardization, Quality Assurance, Metrology and Testing Act, 2006 (EAC SQMT Act, 2006) in 2006. Based on this Act, the EAC has started to harmonize standards, with priority given to the top 20 major intra-regional trading goods, including fish products. Since the East African Standard (EAS) takes precedence over national regulations and standards, member countries are obliged to adopt the EAC standard[23] (Will, 2012: 34). As a member of the EAC, Tanzania must follow the decisions of the East African Standards Commission (EASC), which is responsible for developing harmonized regional standards.[24] Because the degree of economic integration of the EAC is more advanced than other RECs, the degree of harmonization of the regulations and standards is high. Therefore, the revision procedure is time-consuming and requires the consent of other countries.[25]

Both COMESA and the SADC have been promoting harmonization of SPS measures within the region respectively. The Regulations on the Application of Sanitary and Phytosanitary Measures (COMESA SPS Regulations) was adopted by the COMESA Council and entered into force in 2009.[26] On the other hand, the SADC Protocol on Trade stipulates that member countries should base SPS measures on international standards, guidelines, and recommendations in order to harmonize SPS measures among members (Article 16) (Chinyamakobvu 2017: 21). Although these RECs have advocated for the harmonization of SPS rules, both COMESA SPS Regulations and the SADC Protocol on Trade did not exist at the time when the EU introduced the hygiene package. Even if they did exist, they have less impact when Madagascar and Mauritius enhanced their SPS measures in response to the EU hygiene package. The reason for this is that the COMESA SPS Regulations and the SADC Protocol on Trade have the same characteristics as the WTO SPS Agreement, which does not specify the SPS measures, but rather establishes the basic operating rules for SPS measures. In that sense, the harmonization of fish standards implemented at the SADC as the Fish-Trade Project started in 2015 may affect the speed at which EU regulations on food safety diffuse in SADC members (Hlatshwayo et al., 2017: 24; Landell Mills 2020: 18).

4.5   CONCLUSION

This comparative study on fishery policy among three African fish-exporting countries has clarified that even the same regulations have different impacts on each country's regulatory frameworks. The diffusion mechanisms of regulations regarding fishery products vary depending on the characteristics of regulation, the degree of importance of market access, and the existence of regional laws.

Since food safety measures, especially in developed countries, which are significant export markets, are being continuously revised and strengthened, it is still a large challenge for developing countries. Whenever the EU has changed and upgraded its food safety standards and regulations, Tanzania, Madagascar, and Mauritius have introduced or tried to introduce the EU's new standards on fishery products. If they do not, these countries will lose an important exporting market. To maintain or to increase their exports to the EU, these countries must meet the current and future food safety requirements of their export markets. In this sense, coercion and/or competition is the basic motivating factor for all three of these African countries to reform their own legal system in order to comply with EU regulations.

However, there is a difference among these three countries on how each has proactively adopted these new EU regulations; each has had a different degree of motivation about implementing these changes. The decision to follow the EU policy primarily depends on the importance of the fishery sector in each country. The more important the EU market is to the country, such as Mauritius in this case, the more quickly it will respond to the new EU requirements. The presence of regional standards also influences the speed at which a country may adopt these regulations. If there are regional standards that are harmonized and actually implemented among the members of a regional organization, the country, such as Tanzania in this case, needs more time to modify its standards so that they can meet EU requirements.

This study has also found that actions from the leader countries who set new regulations significantly influence follower countries, who accept the relevant new regulations. In other words, the EU regularly audits Tanzania, Madagascar, and Mauritius to assess their compliance with the new regulations, which resulted in accelerating their regulatory modification. Interactions between the EU and three African countries is one of the important factors that influence the speed of policy diffusion.

NOTES

1. The literature on the impact of standards on international trade are numerous. The majority of these studies have concluded that standards and SPS measures act to impede trade because developing countries generally have "inadequate development of science and technology, institutions, management, absorptive capacity of producers, … which prevent them from conforming to the standards in the markets of their trading partners, particularly the developed countries" (Kareem, 2016: 87). However, some studies have stated that standards have trade promoting or trade diverting effects in the long run (Kareem, 2016: 87; Murina and Nicita, 2014: 1).
2. For example, since it is difficult to clearly determine definitions of terms such as "food" for the purposes of the legislation, the definitions in the CODEX materials are effectively applied to national legislations in some countries (WHO, 2017: 28).
3. It was on the fishery products that HACCP was first widely applied. Whereas the EU introduced HACCP controls for the safety of live bivalve mollusks and fish products in 1991, the US Food and Drug Administration mandated all processors selling fishery products in the US to adopt HACCP (Donovan et al., 2001: 164).
4. Interviews with an official of the Tanzania Bureau of Standards, October 2017, officials of Ministry for Agriculture and Fisheries, Madagascar, October 2017, and an official of the Competent Authority Seafood, Mauritius, October 2017.
5. The EU provided a transition period of two years from 2004 for the new rules to be applied smoothly. During this period, governments were allowed to implement certain requirements progressively (Neeliah et al., 2011: 61; Reilly, 2007: 48).
6. The European Commission Regulation (1881/2006) specifies maximum levels for a number of contaminants in food, including some persistent organic pollutants, metals, mycotoxins, process contaminants, and polycyclic aromatic hydrocarbons (Food Safety Authority of Ireland, 2014: 3). In the case of marine products, the contaminants subject to regulation include lead, cadmium, mercury, dioxins, and melamine.

7. Regulation (1333/2008) on food additives sets the rules on food additives stipulating that all additives in the EU must be authorized and be used in the form of a positive list with the labeling requirement (Food Safety Authority of Ireland, 2015: 3).
8. Concerning containers and packaging for foods, framework Regulation (1935/2004) on materials and articles intended to come into contact with food stipulates that "[m]aterials and articles, including active and intelligent materials and articles, shall be manufactured in compliance with good manufacturing practice" (Article 3) (Karamfilova, 2016: 14).
9. See the leaflet published by the EU titled "EU import conditions for seafood and other fishery products." Retrieved from https://ec.europa.eu/food/sites/food/files/safety/docs/ia_trade_import-cond-fish_en.pdf (last accessed August 2020).
10. See the leaflet mentioned above.
11. https://ec.europa.eu/food/audits-analysis/audit_reports/index.cfm (last accessed August 2020).
12. It has a provision for sustainable development, protection, conservation, aquaculture development, regulation and control of fish and fishery products, aquatic flora and its products, and other related matters.
13. For example, one project analyzing the legal framework of Madagascar supported by the EU in 2005 identified some gaps and weaknesses hindering proper monitoring, control, and surveillance in the marine fisheries sector, such as inspections, observer systems, transshipment, compounding procedures, classification of violations, and penalties. On this basis, Madagascar began the legal drafting process in the same year that the report was issued (Breuil and Grima, 2014: 27).
14. Interview with an official of the Ministry of Agriculture, Livestock, and Fisheries, October 2018.
15. Website of Ministry of Blue Economy, Marine Resources, Fisheries and Shipping. Retrieved from http://blueconomy.govmu.org/English/Pages/Fisheries—10-Year-Fisheries-Development-Plan.aspx (last accessed August 2020).
16. The regulation (No. 27 of 2006) has been replaced by the subsequent regulation, the Fisheries and Marine Resources (Export of Fish and Fish Products) Regulations (No. 2) 2006 (Government Notice No. 148 of 2006).
17. Because Tanzania has three international lakes—Lake Victoria, Lake Tanganyika, and Lake Nyasa—the fishery products taken from inland waters are large. Although the marine fishery has a vast watershed, since the continental shelf is narrow, the fishery is limited to specific coastal areas.
18. The share of fish exports rose from 7.5% in 1997 to 13.5% in 2003.
19. The rest are sea farming (5%) and freshwater production (25%).
20. The EAC consists of six countries: Burundi, Kenya, Rwanda, South Sudan, Tanzania, and Uganda.
21. The SADC consists of 16 countries: Angola, Botswana, Comoros, Democratic Republic of Congo, Eswatini, Lesotho, Madagascar, Malawi, Mauritius, Mozambique, Namibia, Seychelles, South Africa, Tanzania, Zambia, and Zimbabwe.
22. COMESA consists of 21 countries: Burundi, Comoros, Democratic Republic of Congo, Djibouti, Egypt, Eritrea, Eswatini, Ethiopia, Kenya, Libya, Madagascar, Malawi, Mauritius, Rwanda, Seychelles, Somalia, Sudan, Tunisia, Uganda, Zambia, and Zimbabwe.
23. Article 15(1) of the EAC SQMT Act, 2006 provides that "the Partner States shall adopt, without deviation from the approved text of the standard, the East African

Standard as a national standard and withdraw any existing national standard with similar scope and purpose."

24. Interview with an official of the Tanzania Bureau of Standards, October 2017, and an official of the EAC Secretariat, October 2018.
25. A draft EAS is circulated to stakeholders including government, private sectors, and consumer groups through the respective national standards bodies of the member countries. Comments received are discussed and incorporated, if needed, before the standard is finalized (interview with an official of the EAC Secretariat, October 2018).
26. The main purpose of the COMESA SPS Regulations is the implementation of the WTO SPS Agreement at the COMESA regional level (Ravelomanantsoa, 2012: 20). The COMESA SPS Regulations was modeled after the WTO SPS Agreement, and the COMESA member countries have to enact the COMESA SPS Regulations as a domestic law, so once the COMESA SPS Regulations comes into force, countries that are not WTO members also implement WTO SPS Agreement in their jurisdiction.

REFERENCES

Ayalew, H., Birhanu, A., and Asrade, B. (2013). Review on food safety system: Ethiopian perspective. *African Journal of Food Science*, 7(12), 431–40. doi: 10.5897/AJFS2013.1064

Barendsz, A.W. (1998). Food safety and total quality management. *Food Control*, 9(2–3), 163–70. doi: 10.1016/S0956-7135(97)00074-1

Breuil, C., and Grima, D. (2014). Baseline report Madagascar. Smartfish programme of the Indian Ocean commission, fisheries management FAO component. Ebene, Mauritius, pp. 1–35. Retrieved from http://www.fao.org/3/a-br796e.pdf (last accessed August 2020).

Chinyamakobvu, O.S. (2017). The Technical Barriers to Trade (TBT) and Sanitary and Phytosanitary (SPS) Policies of African Regional Economic Communities (RECs). Nairobi, Kenya: Pan-African Quality Infrastructure (PAQI). Retrieved from http://www.paqi.org/wp-content/uploads/2014/09/PAQI_TBT_SPS_2017_english_web.pdf (last accessed August 2020).

Competent Authority of Tanzania (CAT) (2006). Response of the competent authority of TANZANIA to the recommendations of mission report ref. DG (SANCO). 8241/2006. Retrieved from http://ec.europa.eu/food/fvo/ap/ap_tanzania_8241_2006.pdf (last accessed August 2020).

Czubala, W., Shepherd, B., and Wilson, J.S. (2009). Help or hindrance? The impact of harmonised standards on African exports. *Journal of African Economies*, 18(5), 711–44. doi:10.1093/jae/ejp003

Daby, P (2003). A critical view of the fish processing sector in Mauritius with particular reference to seafood safety and quality assurance. UNU-Fisheries Training Programme, United Nations Educational, Scientific and Cultural Organization (UNESCO). Retrieved from https://www.grocentre.is/static/gro/publication/130/document/daby03prf.pdf (last accessed November 2020).

Day, R., Tambi, E., and Odularu, G. (2012). An analysis of compliance with selected sanitary and phytosanitary measures in eastern and southern Africa. Accra, Ghana: Forum for Agricultural Research in Africa (FARA).

Donovan, J.A., Caswell, J.A., and Salay, E. (2001). The effect of stricter foreign regulations on food safety levels in developing countries: A study of Brazil. *Review of Agricultural Economics*, 23(1), 163–75.

Food and Agriculture Organization of the United Nations (FAO) (2014). Country Programming Framework for Mauritius, 2014–2017. Retrieved from http://www.fao.org/3/a-bp618e.pdf (last accessed November 2020).

Food and Agriculture Organization of the United Nations (FAO) and World Trade Organization (WTO) (2017). Trade and Food Standards. Retrieved from http://www.fao.org/3/a-i7407e.pdf (last accessed August 2020).

Food and Veterinary Office (FVO) (2005). Extract from a report concerning a visit by the Food and Veterinary Office to Madagascar from 21 February to 4 March 2005 to assess the conditions for the production and export of fishery and aquaculture products to the European Union. Audit Reports, DG(SANCO)/7553/2005—RS EN, Health and Consumer Protection Directorate-General. Retrieved from https://ec.europa.eu/food/audits-analysis/audit_reports/details.cfm?rep_id=1311 (last accessed August 2020).

Food and Veterinary Office (FVO) (2006a). Final report of a mission carried out in Mauritius from 23 to 27 January 2006 in order to assess the public health controls and the conditions of production of fishery products. Audit Reports, DG(SANCO)/8155/2006—MR Final, Health and Consumer Protection Directorate-General. Retrieved from https://ec.europa.eu/food/audits-analysis/audit_reports/details.cfm?rep_id=1550 (last accessed August 2020).

Food and Veterinary Office (FVO) (2006b). Final report of a mission carried out in Tanzania from 25 September to 6 October 2006 in order to assess the public health controls and the conditions of production of fishery products. Audit Reports, DG(SANCO)/8241/2006—MR Final, Health and Consumer Protection Directorate-General. Retrieved from https://ec.europa.eu/food/audits-analysis/audit_reports/details.cfm?rep_id=1625 (last accessed August 2020).

Food and Veterinary Office (FVO) (2007). Final report of a follow-up mission carried out in Madagascar from 1 to 9 March 2007 in order to evaluate the control systems in place governing the production of fishery and aquaculture products intended for export to the European Union. Audit Reports, DG(SANCO)/2007-7302—MR Final, Health and Consumer Protection Directorate-General. Retrieved from https://ec.europa.eu/food/audits-analysis/audit_reports/details.cfm?rep_id=1809 (last accessed November 2020).

Food and Veterinary Office (FVO) (2008). Final report of a mission carried out in Mauritius from 05 February to 14 February 2008 in order to evaluate the control systems in place governing the production of fishery products intended for export to the European Union (follow up). Audit Reports, DG(SANCO)/2008-7668—MR Final, Health and Consumer Protection Directorate-General. Retrieved from https://ec.europa.eu/food/audits-analysis/audit_reports/details.cfm?rep_id=1990 (last accessed August 2020).

Food Safety Authority of Ireland (2014). Legislation on chemical contaminants. Retrieved from https://www.fsai.ie/publications_chemical_contaminants/ (last accessed August 2020).

Food Safety Authority of Ireland (2015). Guidance on food additives revision 2, 2015. Retrieved from https://www.fsai.ie/guidanceonfoodadditivesrevision12011.html (last accessed August 2020).

Henson, S., Brouder, A., and Mitullah, W. (2000). Food safety requirements and food exports from developing countries: The case of fish exports from Kenya to the European Union. *American Journal of Agricultural Economics*, 82(5), 1159–69.

Hlatshwayo, H., Molapo, K., Lungu, M., and Chimatiro, S. (2017). Improving food security and reducing poverty through intra-regional fish trade. *Inside SADC* (SADC Secretariat Monthly Newsletter), 8, 24–5. Retrieved from https://www.sadc.int/files/8815/0479/0760/Inside_SADC_August_2017.pdf (last accessed August 2020).

Humber, F., Andriamahefazafy, M., Godley, B.J., and Broderick, A.C. (2015). Endangered, essential and exploited: How extant laws are not enough to protect marine megafauna in Madagascar. *Marine Policy*, 60, 70–83. doi: 10.1016/j.marpol.2015.05.006

Jukes, D.J. (1988). Developing a food control system: The Tanzanian experience. *Food Policy*, 13(3), 293-304. doi: 10.1016/0306-9192(88)90051-6

Karamfilova, E. (2016). Food contact materials regulation (EC) 1935/2004: European implementation assessment study. European Parliamentary Research Service (EPRS). Retrieved from https://www.europarl.europa.eu/RegData/etudes/STUD/2016/581411/EPRS_STU%282016%29581411_EN.pdf (last accessed August 2020).

Kareem, O.I. (2016). European Union's standards and food exports from Africa: Implications of the comprehensive Africa Agricultural Development Programme for coffee and fish. *Journal of African Development*, 18(1), 83–97.

Landell Mills (2020). Final evaluation of the FishTrade Project Improving Food Security and Reducing Poverty through intraregional fish trade in sub-Saharan Africa (FishTrade) implemented by WorldFish, Final report. Retrieved from https://digitalarchive.worldfishcenter.org/bitstream/handle/20.500.12348/4090/d78e8e519a763bed9912c4cc45cfbdd8.pdf (last accessed August 2020).

Lee, R.U., and Namisi, P. (2016). Baseline study on Tanzania fisheries: Draft final report. Danish Ministry of Foreign Affairs.

Minister of Agro Industry and Fisheries, Republic of Mauritius (MOAIF) (2008). A Sustainable Diversified Agri-Food Sector Strategy for Mauritius, 2008–2015. Retrieved from https://sustainabledevelopment.un.org/content/documents/1250maurFood%20Security%20Strategy.pdf (last accessed November 2020).

Ministry of Agriculture, Livestock, and Fisheries, United Republic of Tanzania (2016). *The Tanzanian Fisheries Sector: Challenges and Opportunities*. Dar es Salaam, United Republic of Tanzania: Author.

Ministry of Industry, Trade and Marketing, United Republic of Tanzania (2011). Project Proposal for Implementation as part of Trade Sector Development Programme (TSDP), Final version. Retrieved from https://www.standardsfacility.org/sites/default/files/STDF_PPG_268_ProjectDocument_Feb-11.pdf (last accessed August 2020).

Murina, M., and Nicita, A. (2014). Trading with conditions: The effect of sanitary and phytosanitary measures on lower income countries' agricultural exports. *Policy Issues in International Trade and Commodities Research Study Series*, 68. UNCTAD. Retrieved from https://unctad.org/en/PublicationsLibrary/itcdtab70_en.pdf (last accessed August 2020).

Neeliah, H., and Neeliah, S.A. (2014). Changing agro-food export composition and SPS compliance: Lessons for Mauritius. *The Estey Centre Journal of International Law and Trade Policy*, 15(1), 92–114. doi: 10.22004/ag.econ.244587.

Neeliah, S.A., Neeliah, H., and Goburdhun, D. (2011). Sanitary and phytosanitary issues for fishery exports to the European Union: A Mauritian insight. *Journal of Development and Agricultural Economics*, 3(2), 56–68.

Neeliah, S.A., Neeliah, H., and Goburdhun, D. (2013). Assessing the relevance of EU SPS measures to the food export sector: Evidence from a developing agro-food exporting country. *Food Policy*, 41, 53–62. Retrieved from https://reader.elsevier.com/reader/sd/pii/S030691921300033X?token=1A2567C4B8 07F176A2D7C12EE0E201D1DAF7890ACC72126F029CFE93A8F097091D5 94713C771B4EAF18D1C7DB98CFD5D (last accessed August 2020).

Orden, D., and Roberts, D. (2007). Food regulation and trade under the WTO: Ten years in perspective. *Agricultural Economics*, 37(1), 103–18. doi: 10.1111/j.1574-0862.2007.00238.x

Ravelomanantsoa, L. (2012). Legal Study on the Regulations on the Application of Sanitary and Phytosanitary Measures of the Common Market for Eastern and Southern Africa. The National Legal Implications of the COMESA Green Pass Certification Scheme. Retrieved from https://www.standardsfacility.org/sites/default/files/STDF_PPG_346_FinalLegalStudy_Jun-12.pdf (last accessed August 2020).

Reilly, A. (2007). From farm to fork—new European food hygiene regulations. In H. Einarsson, and W. Emerson (eds), *International Seafood Trade: Challenges and Opportunities*. FAO/University of Akureyri Symposium, February 1–2, 2007, Akureyri, Iceland. FAO Fisheries and Aquaculture Proceedings, No. 13. Rome: FAO, pp. 47–56. Retrieved from http://www.fao.org/3/a-i0584e.pdf (last accessed August 2020).

Wahidin, D., and Purnhagen, K. (2018). Improving the level of food safety and market access in developing countries. *Heliyon*, 4(7), 1–24. doi: 10.1016/j.heliyon.2018.e00683

Will, M. (2012). Harmonisation and mutual recognition of regulations and standards for food safety and quality in regional economic communities: The case of the East African Community (EAC) and the Common Market for Eastern and Southern Africa (COMESA). Bonn, Germany: Deutsche Gesellschaft für Internationale Zusammenarbeit (GIZ).

World Health Organization (WHO) (2012). An overview of national Codex Committees in the Member States of the WHO South-East Asia Region. Retrieved from https://apps.who.int/iris/rest/bitstreams/912744/retrieve (last accessed August 2020).

World Health Organization (WHO) (2017). Food Safety and Nutrition Food Law Guidelines. Retrieved from https://www.afro.who.int/sites/default/files/2017-06/Food%20Safety%20and%20Nutrition%20Food%20Law%20Guidelines.pdf (last accessed August 2020).

5. Seeking the similarities while keeping the differences: the development of emissions trading schemes in northeast Asia

Fang-Ting Cheng

5.1 INTRODUCTION

Emissions trading schemes (ETSs) are a market-based approach to reducing greenhouse gas (GHG) emissions in response to climate change. Pioneered by the US and the European Union (EU), ETSs have been established in European countries, the US, and Asian developing countries (Bang et al., 2017; Schmalensee and Stavins, 2013; Skjærseth and Wettestad, 2008). Policy diffusion studies have generally focused on regulations or policies from the center of one source that are gradually diffused to other jurisdictions (Biedenkopf et al., 2017b). This chapter examines the development of ETSs from a similar perspective. To date, ETSs have been established in China, the Republic of Korea (hereafter Korea), Kazakhstan, and New Zealand; Japan has implemented a national voluntary credit system; and Taiwan, Thailand, and Vietnam are considering the introduction of an ETS (ICAP, 2017, 2018). Development in East Asian countries deserves greater attention as carbon markets were introduced in the early 2000s, with the Chinese national ETS being one of the largest.

Although inspired by early pioneer regulations or policies, many ETSs have been modified to fit local-specific political, economic, social, and institutional contexts (Bang et al., 2017; Biedenkopf et al., 2017a, 2017b) as carbon market policy instruments cannot be simply copied from one jurisdiction to another (Knox-Hayes, 2016). However, as mentioned in previous research, the interactions between the different schemes in different jurisdictions need greater elaboration (Biedenkopf et al., 2017a), especially as there are currently wide-ranging discussions on the establishment of an international carbon market.

Therefore, instead of focusing on the diffusion mechanism or process of ETSs, this chapter highlights the outcomes of diffusion and examines how countries respond to the consequences. Although the above-mentioned integration has been advocated by international organizations such as the World Bank (Bang et al., 2017: 20), the fragmented country-based ETS systems have meant that there are considerable difficulties in integrating these markets, which is why ETS links across specific regions have been limited. There is also the view that linking ETS markets would only increase complications and could result in greater inefficiency and uncertainty (Green, 2017).

Since ETSs have developed in different ways in respective jurisdictions, policy convergence, regarded as an outcome often accompanied by policy diffusion, has become very inconspicuous (Biedenkopf et al., 2017b). Some stakeholders see value in "linking the markets" to ensure overall environmental integrity (to prevent carbon leakage) and efficiency (emissions reduction costs) (Ewing, 2016, 2017). This raises the question of how different systems could be integrated; furthermore, the motivation for countries to converge when faced with challenges must also be considered.

To date, such questions have not yet received much attention and analysis in the literature on policy diffusion in ETS. Along with the expansion of ETSs in Asia, countries are introducing experimental forms of ETS with some discussion on mutual linkage even though the schemes are considerably different. China launched its national ETS in 2018, after the announcement in 2017; it is, as previously mentioned, the world's largest carbon market in terms of regulated carbon emissions (Han et al., 2012; ICAP, 2018). Korea launched a national ETS, the K-ETS; the first phase started in 2015 and ended in 2017. Japan introduced its voluntary emissions trading scheme (JVETS) in 2005, which finished its seventh phase in 2013. Policy makers in these countries have consistently claimed that they are in support of a more harmonized market in the future.

Specific research questions based on empirical studies can be raised here: why have northeast Asian countries, according to their circumstances, introduced different ETSs while still searching for a common carbon pricing mechanism? More specifically, from a theoretical perspective: if the establishment of mutual linkages and a common market involves such barriers because of the different scopes of the individual ETSs, what motivates these countries to continue multilateral conversations and to cooperate by sharing each other's experiences? This chapter focuses on the ETSs in China, Korea, and Japan, analyzing how countries respond to the outcomes of diffusion from the perspective of policy learning, as these countries have been making efforts to develop a common vision despite their individual schemes differing substantially (Central Environment Council Global Environment Subcommittee, 2018; World Bank, 2016).

The reason this chapter focuses on China, Korea, and Japan is because the three countries have been working together to assess the viability of region-wide integration. Despite the fact that the Chinese ETS will be the biggest carbon market, these countries have invariably promoted GHG emissions trading schemes in recent years; but these countries have been developing highly heterogeneous systems while aiming to coordinate and integrate with those of other countries in the region. As a widely spread policy tool to address climate change, the diffusion of ETS shows diversity in the process of policy diffusion (Betsill and Hoffmann, 2011; Biedenkopf et al., 2017b; Paterson et al., 2014).

In the following sections, policy diffusion in each country is outlined with a focus on the reasons for the differences in the regulations compared with the pioneers, after which a comparison of the differences in the Chinese, Korean, and Japanese ETSs is conducted. After clarifying the domestic barriers to ETS, the motivations for maintaining cooperation on linkages or more harmonized markets are analyzed based on the current multilateral discussions.

5.2   POLICY DIFFUSION OF ETS AT THE INTERNATIONAL LEVEL

As analyzed in the introduction and in other chapters, policy diffusion, which is defined as the spread of innovative policies beyond jurisdictions, has been observed in many policy areas, and particularly in environmental policies (e.g. Busch et al., 2005; Daley and Garand, 2005; Dolšak and Sampson, 2012; Tews and Busch, 2001; Tews et al., 2003). Unlike policy transfers, when policies are transferred from one individual jurisdiction to another, policy diffusion involves transfers from one jurisdiction to multiple jurisdictions (Biedenkopf et al., 2017b: 92; Holzinger et al., 2007: 13–17). However, policy diffusion does not necessarily mean "copying a policy" as the regulations across jurisdictions can be different in terms of administration, technology, scope, and ambition (Busch et al., 2005). Many environmental regulations, for example, have been diffused into other jurisdictions with modifications (Cheng et al., 2017).

We believe that the development of ETSs is an outcome of policy diffusion. To address climate change challenges, these market-based instruments have diffused at different levels across regions (Newell et al., 2013; Redmond and Convery, 2015; Underdal et al., 2015). Paterson et al. argued that it was best described as a case of polycentric diffusion where the various ETSs "all serve similar goals under a broad policy framework guided loosely by the UN-based climate regime" (Paterson et al., 2014: 420). However, the policies or regulations adopted are altered to reflect domestic concerns based on the needs and wants of the various interests of diverse stakeholders (Müller and Slominski,

2016, 2017; Wettestad and Gulbrandsen, 2017). Betsill and Hoffmann found that ETSs had been widely implemented as policy tools to address climate change, but the different jurisdictions had made diverse modifications or adjustments (Betsill and Hoffmann, 2011).

One of the reasons for ETS system heterogeneity has been a concern for market stability, particularly when there had been unsuccessful experiences in other jurisdictions (Bang et al., 2017), which is also why countries have tended to first launch pilot projects or voluntary programs before the full introduction of a national program (Biedenkopf et al., 2017b; Munnings et al., 2014). For example, until 2017 China had seven pilot projects, Korea's K-ETS has short operating phases of only two years so that policy makers can quickly respond to the problems or market failures and subsequently correct the system in a timely manner, and Japan implemented a voluntary national ETS to accumulate experience and feedback. Therefore, to ensure that the ETSs are suitable for local conditions, it has been necessary to experiment with and then adjust the system over time.

ETS diffusion research has noted that countries that have introduced ETSs have usually modified the schemes by setting different scopes, rules, coverage, and so on, or by developing innovative new arrangements based on their respective conditions such as external finance intentions, domestic policy motivations, broker self-interest, political will, and differing capacities (Bang et al., 2017; Biedenkopf et al., 2017a, 2017b; Müller and Slominski, 2017). Therefore, rather than copying the EU or other pioneer ETSs, other countries are generally tending to initially implement trial programs at the national or sub-national level to test the waters. For example, before the national ETS was launched, China had seven pilot projects to gather experience and feed back results to central government policy makers (Biedenkopf et al., 2017a).

In contrast, although they are still being debated, international environmental agreements have provided the basis for policy diffusion in the establishment and connection of ETSs. Since the Kyoto Protocol was adopted in 1997 under the United Nations Framework Convention on Climate Change (UNFCCC), the number of carbon markets has increased to 21 under 28 jurisdictions at different levels including sub-national (states, provinces, or municipalities), national, and supranational institutions (ICAP, 2017, 2018). The UNFCCC Paris Agreement took effect in 2016, opening up a new era for tackling serious climate change through common global guidelines and principles.

Under the Paris Agreement, voluntarily introduced market-based methods are regarded as one of the possible ways to efficiently reduce GHG emissions. The Agreement stated that:

> Parties shall, where engaging on a voluntary basis in cooperative approaches that involve the use of "internationally transferred mitigation outcomes" toward

nationally determined contributions, promote sustainable development and ensure environmental integrity and transparency, including in governance, and shall apply robust accounting to ensure, inter alia, the avoidance of double counting, consistent with guidance adopted by the Conference of the Parties serving as the meeting of the Parties to the Paris Agreement. (Article 6.2 of the Paris Agreement, 2015)

In other words, to achieve the mitigation goals of the Agreement, Parties can transfer their reduced emissions (e.g. as credits) through appropriate methods to other Parties to attain their goals. The mitigation outcomes can be voluntarily transferred internationally, while ensuring environmental integrity and transparency and avoiding a double counting of the Parties' mitigation outcomes. However, of the 21 operating ETSs, very few have mechanisms for connecting to another's market. Since 2014, the State of California in the US and Canada's Quebec (Ontario from 2018) have linked their cap-and-trade programs[1] by permitting any of the jurisdictions to use allowances (allowed to emit) interchangeably for compliance. Allowances can also be auctioned jointly across the programs. These three cap-and-trade programs all belong to the Western Climate Initiative (WCI), which was designed based on a common template to link these markets.

5.3   ANALYTICAL PERSPECTIVE: LEARNING AFTER DIFFUSION

"Diffusion through learning" has been widely discussed as one mechanism in the literatures on policy diffusion (e.g. Gilardi, 2010, 2012; Jörgens, 2004; Kern et al., 2005; Meseguer, 2005; Shipan and Volden, 2008). For example, Underdal argues that "diffusion happened by learning from errors rather than by simply copying" (Underdal, 2013). Gilardi also pointed out that policy makers, with a focus on the patterns and process of diffusion, can learn from others' successful experiences rationally to reduce uncertainty (Gilardi, 2012: 464). However, "learning can be imperfect, conditional on ideology," since "policy makers learn selectively from the available evidence concerning both the policy and political consequences of reforms" (Gilardi, 2012: 466, 471). On the case of emissions trading, these findings also provide explanations for why countries learn from the pioneers' successful experiences but introduced different policies of reform based on self-interests.

Previous research on policy diffusion of ETS has similarly focused on the process and learning behaviors from pioneers before jurisdictions introduce a new policy (Gilardi, 2012; Inderberg et al., 2017; Müller and Slominski, 2016, 2017). As was seen in the ETS developments in northeast Asia, it is true that the countries gradually introduced ETS by learning from others through experimentation and by themselves through trial and error, as self-learning has also been observed in northeast Asia to be a key factor influencing decision making (Gulbrandsen et al., 2017). However, as mentioned in the introduction, the outcome of diffusion (which means after diffusion) and how countries react to the divergence of policies reform need more theoretical consideration. This is because the imperfect outcomes caused by policy diffusion inevitably need to be improved, and there will still be great uncertainty as well as other challenges in the continuous process of reform.

In order to answer the questions raised in the introduction, we firstly clarify the causes for, and the rationality of, the different regulations in China, Korea, and Japan; secondly, we explain their motivations and goals, and elucidate the reasons why these countries are seeking possibilities to cooperate on linking systems or developing a more integrated market despite the crucial differences in basic ETS design. As the economic merits and motivations have been broadly discussed in many other studies, this chapter focuses on the policy and political motivations in dealing with current systematical divergence. Learning should not only be regarded as one important mechanism of policy diffusion, as argued and analyzed in previous researches, but also be treated, at least for ETS cases, as a key approach to meet the above-mentioned policy and political motivations after diffusion.

Through policy learning, China, Korea, and Japan carefully developed ETSs in a phased experimental method, which also caused heterogeneity between systems. The Chinese national ETS was launched in 2018, the pilot projects and their associated trading agency are to continue parallel operations with the national ETS, to update and report on their trading situations, and give feedback on the obstacles to both local and central governments.[2]

The Korean ETS has been operating since 2015, and though it has short operating phases of two years, it is still regarded as a carbon trading market. Before the official operations were launched, Korea had introduced a GHG Emissions and Energy Consumption Target Management System (TMS), which was a command and control regulation for government and companies to better understand the GHG emissions status and the "measurement," "reporting," and "verification" (MRV) system. The TMS was divided into three one-year preparatory stage periods, after which new modifications were made based on the experience in the previous preparation period. To maintain system modification flexibility, Phase I and II were covered two-year periods, from 2015 to 2017 and from 2018 to 2020, with the five-year Phase III scheduled to run from 2021 to 2025, at which time it is expected to be linked to other ETSs (Ministry of Environment of Korea, 2018).

Japan also experimentally introduced its national-level voluntary JVETS in 2005, the year the Kyoto Protocol took effect. Each JVETS phase was for one year, with the seventh phase ending in 2012. This was followed by the voluntary J-Credit Scheme in 2013, which was specifically focused on small and medium-sized enterprises, farmers, forest owners, and municipalities but did not involve the heavy emitters such as steel and automobile manufacturers or power producers. The Cabinet decision on the Plan for Global Warming Countermeasures released in May 2016 indicated that the Japanese government is taking a cautious stance on launching a mandatory national ETS because of strong manufacturing and industry stakeholder power and a fear of losing global competitiveness (Central Environment Council Global Environment Subcommittee, 2018; Ministry of the Environment of Japan, 2016).

Nevertheless, even though it has no national trading scheme yet, Japan has been active in cooperating on the possibility of a cross-border ETS by facilitating conversation, knowledge sharing, and capacity building under the initiative of the Japanese Ministry of Environment (MOEJ) with China and Korea. In contrast to the relatively negative attitude of the national Japanese government on a national ETS, Tokyo (followed by Saitama and Kyoto) launched a sub-national ETS in 2010, which was the first installed metropolitan scheme. Having similar scopes, the Tokyo and Saitama ETSs decided to link their markets through the trading and co-use of credits from 2014.

In the following sections, the commonalities and differences in the northeast Asian ETSs are explored in more detail to assess the fundamental design challenges for an integrated market. That is, through comparison, the fundamental differences in the systems can highlight the difficulties and challenges of direct linkage between markets.

5.4   THE FRAGMENTATION OF ETSs IN NORTHEAST ASIA

Unlike the ETSs in the US and Canadian states under the WCI framework, the diffusion in northeast Asia is fragmented, where the national and sub-national carbon markets were introduced with different goals and institutional designs. However, even though there are many differences, it is expected that these markets should be linked within and possibly outside the region (e.g. the Asia Society Policy Institute; Carbon Pricing Leadership Coalition; World Bank Group's Networked Carbon Markets Initiative) (Zhou et al., 2018). It should be noted that linking carbon markets requires policy convergence as it would require an integrated basic system design (e.g. scope, coverage, MRV), standards of integrity (e.g. additionality, sustainability, transparency), rigorous review mechanisms, and so on (Ewing and Shin, 2017). As there is no international overarching framework, building a common market is challenging.

In this section, the commonalities and differences in ETSs are explored in more detail in terms of their emissions reduction targets, scopes, nature, and coverage. Therefore, in this chapter a considerable amount of space is spent to understand the differences in system design between markets. This part focuses on national ETSs and the challenges and possibilities of interconnections between the markets at a national level. Table 5.1 shows the outcome of the comparisons.

5.4.1   Emissions Reduction Target

The emissions reduction target determines the expected GHGs emissions reduction from the ETS operations in each jurisdiction. Under the Paris Agreement, Parties must submit their nationally determined contributions (NDCs) every five years to the Secretariat of UNFCCC along with their emissions reduction targets and other efforts being made to achieve these objectives (Article 3 of the Paris Agreement, 2015[3]). For example, the EU has pledged to reduce GHG emissions by 40% of 1990 levels by 2030. hina has pledged to reduce CO_2 emissions per unit of gross domestic product (GDP) by 60–65% of 2005 levels and peak-out its CO_2 emissions by 2030, Korea has pledged to reduce emissions by 37% from business-as-usual (BaU)[4] levels by 2030, and Japan, a developed country, has pledged a 26% reduction in GHG emissions by 2030 from 2013 levels.

The heterogeneity of emissions reduction targets affects the purpose of each ETS and the allocation of emission allowance. Different from numerous absolute emissions reduction targets submitted by Korean and Japanese governments, China, as a developing country, intends to implement an intensity target, which means although the emissions intensity is to decrease, the overall emissions may increase (Xiong and Qi, 2015). As China has adopted a cap-and-trade approach for its national ETS, it was seen as necessary to convert its emissions intensity reduction target to an absolute emissions reduction target in advance to avoid "over-allocation" or "liquidity" problems[5] (Mattei, 2018). China's national cap-and-trade ETS is going to allocate emissions allowances for free in its first phase, as was done in the Korean K-ETS; however, as there is no mandatory ETS in Japan, there are no allocation problems.

Each country has different national reduction targets, allocation methods, and base years, which further increases the barriers to future market linkages. Also, each country has different ideas and positions on a common emissions reduction target and even toward the role of ETS. The reasons are firstly, China prefers to stabilize its domestic markets; secondly, Korea would prefer to link with China or other ETSs; and thirdly, Japan is struggling to build a national ETS. All in all, while there are common issues, there are also substantial differences such as regional economic disparity, the lack of transnational coordination arrangements, and a lack of integrated reduction targets, all of which makes the possibility of connectedness even more challenging (Carbon Pulse, 2017a, 2017b; Lo, 2013; Lo and Howes, 2013; Zhou et al., 2018).

Table 5.1   *Comparison of basic ETS designs in the EU, China, Korea, and Japan*

	EU-ETS (Phase III) 2013–2020	China National ETS (Phase 1) 2017–2019	China Pilots (2013–)	Korea (Phase I) 2015–2017	Japan JVETS	Japan Tokyo, Saitama, Kyoto
Emissions Reduction Targets	GHG 20% (1990) by 2020; 40% by 2030.	Carbon intensity 40–45% (2005) by 2020; 60–65% by 2030; CO₂ peak-out by 2030		GHG 30% BAU by 2020; 37% BAU by 2030	GHG 25% (2000) by 2020	GHG 30% (2000) by 2030
Allocation	Free allocation and auctioning	Free allocation	Free allocation (except Guangdong)	Free allocation; Future auctioning	N/A	Free allocation
Scope	Supra-national	National	Sub-national	National	National	Sub-national
Liable Entities	>11 000	Up to 1 700	3 332 (seven pilots and Fujian ETS)	599	N/A	1 300 (Tokyo) Up to 600 (Saitama)
Nature	Mandatory	Mandatory	Mandatory	Mandatory; with voluntary opt-in	Voluntary	Mandatory; Voluntary (Kyoto)
Compliance MRV	European Commission Regulation for MRV	Verification Regulation under drafting	Report and third-party verification	Report and third-party verification	Registration, report and third-party verification	Report and third-party verification
Penalties	Excess emissions penalty of €100/tCO₂e ($113/tCO₂e)	Under discussion	Depending on the pilots	Administration fine not exceeding three times the average market price or KRW 100 000/tCO₂e (USD 89)	N/A	A 2-step penalty;[a] No penalty for Saitama ETS
Coverage Sector	Broad range of Industry, including avian	Power generation in Phase 1	Depending on the pilots	Broad range of Industry	Forest, Small-Medium enterprise. Municipality	Office buildings, cooling plant facilities, etc. (Tokyo; Saitama)
Gases	3 GHGs (CO₂, N₂O, PFCs)	CO₂	CO₂; Chongqing: 6 GHGs	6 GHGs (CO₂, CH₄, N₂O, PFCS, HFCs, SF₆)	6 GHGs	CO₂ (Tokyo; Saitama)

Note: [a] 1st step: reduce by 1.3 times the reduction shortfall; 2nd step: if 1st step is not carried out, publicly named, and subjected to penalties (up to JPY 500,000 (USD 4460) and surcharges (1.3 times the shortfall).
Source: ICAP (2017, 2018); https://www.japancredit.go.jp/jcdm/ (accessed November 2020).

5.4.2   Scope

As can be seen in Table 5.1, China recently launched both its national and sub-national ETS pilot projects. Under the national ETS, around 1700 power sector heat and power emitters are to be regulated as well as power plants in other sectors. The Chinese national ETS scope is expected to be enlarged gradually to eventually cover eight sectors; petrochemical, chemical, building materials, steel, nonferrous metals, paper, electricity, and aviation; with both direct emissions from the power sector and indirect emissions from electricity as well as heat consumption being included in the scheme over the long term (ICAP, 2018).

Korea launched K-ETS on January 1, 2015, which was the first nationwide cap-and-trade program in operation in northeast Asia. Similar to the EU-ETS, the K-ETS covers a wide range of sectors and industries, and regulates both the direct emissions of six gases as well as indirect electricity consumption emissions (ICAP, 2018). The first phase of K-ETS was completed at the end of 2017 with 599 reliable entities and five domestic airlines participating. The second phase is from 2018 to 2020, in which 3% of allowances are to be allocated by auctioning and benchmark-based free allocations, covering the following six sectors: heat and power, industry, building, transportation, waste sector, and public. In addition, offsets from international credits developed by domestic companies are allowed to a maximum of 5%, with the number of approved offset project methodologies expected to increase (ICAP, 2018).

Japan has the JVETS, or the J-Credit Scheme; however, participation is voluntary. The J-Credit Scheme was designed to certify the amount of GHG emissions reduced and removed by sinks within Japan. Under the scheme, J-Credit producers are small and medium enterprises, farmers, forest owners, and municipalities, with the consumers being large, small, and medium enterprises, and local governments. The consumers purchase certified J-Credits for multiple purposes such as achieving the Nippon Keidanren's[6] Commitments to a Low Carbon Society, voluntary carbon offsets, and others.

Both national and sub-national ETSs co-exist in China and Japan in the form of domestic offsets. However, the K-ETS is more similar to the EU-ETS, and covers a wider range of sectors, and allows some international offsets with the aim of linking to international carbon markets, especially EU-ETS in the future (Phase III started from 2020). However, there is little need for Japan to trade allowances with other countries for the following reasons: there is no national-level mandatory ETS in Japan; Tokyo and Saitama have already achieved more emissions reductions than expected; and Japan has a modest NDC reduction target. In China, so far the sub-national ETSs are not allowed to trade with other pilots, and the national ETS is still in its initial stages with an expectation to achieve its 2030 reduction target. Through fieldwork and interviews, Chinese policy makers are observed to focus more on building and improving the domestic ETS in the years to come.[7]

5.4.3   Nature

China has launched seven ETS pilot projects and another two ETS at provincial and municipal levels since 2013. Although these pilot projects are experimental, they are mandatory, with emitters under these ETS pilots being required to follow the regulations and accept the compliance rules associated with MRV. As mentioned, China launched its mandatory national ETS in the last days of 2017, which regulates 1700 emitters (entities) from the power sector (see details in coverage). The total regulated GHG emissions is expected to be 3300 $MtCO_2e$ (million metric tons of CO_2 equivalent) per year. If things progress well, the Chinese national ETS is expected to become the world's largest carbon market in terms of regulated carbon emissions (ICAP, 2018). Reporting and MRV by a third-party verifier are required, and noncompliance would result in punishment, although details are under development (ICAP, 2020).

The number of Chinese sub-national ETSs (including seven pilots and two non-pilots) has increased to nine, with Sichuan Province and Fujian Province having launched their carbon markets in December 2016. Parallel with the operation of the national ETS, the sub-national pilot projects continue to trade within their jurisdictions and give feedback to the central government body, formerly the National Development and Reform Commission (NDRC), but now the Ministry of Ecology and the Environment (MEE).The MEE collects the practical experience and feedback from each pilot to develop more detailed rules for its national scheme (Liu, 2018; interview, Tsinghua University and China Beijing Environmental Exchange, 2018[8]). Under the pilot projects and the two local ETSs, compliance (reporting, MRV, and penalties) is enforced at the local level.

Korea has also launched a national ETS, named the K-ETS with phase I running from 2015 to 2017. Different from the Chinese national ETS and the Japanese voluntary ETS, the K-ETS is mandatory and covers a wide range of emitters and gases. The K-ETS is relatively close to a substantial national scheme but is facing a low trading problem (ADB, 2018a). Reporting and MRV by a third-party verifier are required under the scheme; if an entity exceeds its emissions allowances, a penalty is applied that cannot exceed three times the average market price of the allowances in the given compliance year or KRW 100,000/tCO_2e (metric ton of CO_2 equivalent), or approximately US $91/$tCO_2e$.

Japan introduced its voluntary JVETS scheme in 2005, with each new phase being introduced annually; the seventh phase was completed in 2013.

A Japanese national ETS, however, was discussed by the Ministry of the Environment when the Kyoto Protocol took effect in 2008 but is still under consideration because of domestic disputes within the business and industry sectors (Central Environment Council Global Environment Subcommittee, 2018). However, at the sub-national (municipal) level, Tokyo, Saitama, and Kyoto have taken an active stance and launched mandatory ETSs (mandatory: Tokyo and Saitama). Tokyo and Saitama have rigorous reporting and MRV rules and require third-party verifications; a two-step penalty is enforced in cases of noncompliance under the Tokyo ETS (also see Table 5.1); and two ETSs have been linked since 2010.

To date, stakeholders and policy makers are still arguing about the following: the roles the market-based mechanisms such as ETS should play; the design and implementation methods; and the goals for both northeast Asia and other regions (Biedenkopf et al., 2017a). However, even though both China and Korea have mandatory national ETSs, their compliance mechanisms are different, and while Japan has rigorous compliance policies, there is no national-level scheme. Under current international norms, compliance mechanisms have been seen to be the most important factors when establishing a possible common market because it is necessary to ensure the authenticity of the emissions reductions and to prevent double counting (ADB, 2018b; Article 6.2 of the Paris Agreement, 2015). Yet, because of the heterogeneity between ETSs, there also appears to be a long way to go before the emergence of a regionally integrated compliance mechanism.

5.4.4   Coverage (Gases, Sectors, and Thresholds)

The ETS coverage in the three countries varies according to the purpose, the stage of development, and the nature of each scheme. Under Phase I of the Chinese national ETS, only CO_2 and the power sector are regulated, although there are plans to gradually expand the scope to eight sectors. The inclusion thresholds were annual emissions of more than 26,000 tCO_2e or energy consumption of more than 10,000 tce (metric tons of coal equivalent) in any year from 2013 to 2015.

The K-ETS Phase I covered six GHGs (CO_2, CH_4, N_2O, PFC_S, HFCs, and SF_6) and regulated 23 sub-sectors from the steel, cement, petrochemical, refinery, power, construction, waste, and aviation sectors. Phase I covered companies with annual emissions greater than 125,000 tCO_2e, with facilities with annual emissions greater than 25,000 tCO_2e being subject to caps. In addition, companies with annual emissions less than the above-mentioned thresholds were welcomed to voluntarily participate in the K-ETS.

However, in Japan, only CO_2 is regulated in the Tokyo and Saitama ETSs, with entities with annual emissions greater than 13 $MtCO_2e$ in Tokyo and 11

MtCO$_2$e in Saitama being targeted. There are approximately 1300 liable entities in the Tokyo ETS and up to 600 in the Saitama ETS.

Obviously, the sector coverage and inclusion thresholds differ substantially. The K-ETS covers most economic sectors; in Japan, the J-Credit voluntary scheme and the sub-national ETS exclude major emitters such as power plants, transportation, and steel manufacturers; and in the initial phase of China's national ETS, only the power sector is included. There are various reasons for these policy fragmentations, such as the economic development gap, different abatement costs between domestic industries, and attempts to achieve "learning by doing" to avoid repeating the same mistakes (Zhou et al., 2018).

5.5   ANALYSIS: SEEKING A COMMON GROUND WHILE KEEPING THE DIFFERENCES—THE PROSPECTS FOR NORTHEAST ASIAN ETSs

Despite the crucial differences in basic ETS design, China, Korea, and Japan maintain cooperation on carbon pricing. Particularly, even if there are so many institutional differences that a common market in the foreseeable future becomes less possible, why should the three countries still seek cooperation and what motivates them? One thing that can be predicted is that their motivations come from something other than the benefits of the common market itself. This section highlights this development and further analyzes the motivations in detail.

The motivations for continuing cooperation can be understood from the following aspects. The first is to learn from each other and to further build mutual trust. This echoes what Gilardi and other scholars have argued that policy makers can learn rationally to lower uncertainty (e.g. Elkins et al., 2006; Gilardi, 2012; Gilardi et al., 2009; Meseguer, 2009). Maintaining policy roundtables and facilitating dialogue and cooperation provide channels for stakeholders and policy makers to build confidence toward more in-depth cooperation while learning from each other. It is particularly important in northeast Asia, because exploring alternate possibilities could motivate China to improve its MRV capacity, inspire Korea to widen its abatement options, and encourage Japan to launch a national ETS (Ewing, 2017).

One reason reinforcing the above-mentioned motivation is that there are considerable supports for linkages and even for a common northeast Asian carbon market. Linkages can be broadly categorized into fully linking, restricted linking, and indirect linking. However, advocates have also admitted that fully linking and restricted linking would be unlikely in the near future (ASPI, 2018), primarily because the Chinese ETS only covers the power sector and Japan does not have a mandatory national ETS. As mentioned in the previous sections, even indirect linking requires a clear policy direction on the market linkages to capably integrate the different reduction targets, scopes, coverage, and compliance mechanisms (e.g. assurance of the authenticity and credibility of data and MRV report).

Despite the above, there are many other international organizations and communities involved in the promotion of ETSs such as the International Carbon Action Partnership (ICAP) and the Asia Society Policy Institute (ASPI), both supported by the World Bank, which have been taking leadership roles in facilitating policy roundtables in the East Asian region. For example, a meeting was convened by the ASPI, the Carbon Pricing Leadership Coalition, and the World Bank Group's Networked Carbon Markets Initiative on "Exploring East Asian Cooperation on Carbon Markets" among ETS leaders from Japan, China, and Korea at the Carbon Expo in Cologne in May 2016. Also, the Asian Development Bank (ADB) and ICAP launched a regional platform for knowledge sharing on the development and linking of ETS in Asia and the Pacific in Bangkok on November 29, 2016. Furthermore, an ASPI-led policy roundtable, "Carbon Market Cooperation in Northeast Asia," was held in Hong Kong on March 22–23, 2017, and a MOEJ supported symposium on "Market Changes: Making Headway with Carbon Pricing in Asia" was held in Yokohama on July 25, 2017 for policy makers, researchers, and officials of the countries.

For advocates, market links could result in economic (costs reduction), environmental (avoidance of carbon leakages), business (motivations of investment), and strategic (confidence building) benefits (Ewing, 2016, 2017). Linking the markets could increase liquidity, stabilize credit prices, and lower abatement costs and noncompliance risks (ASPI, 2018). This is also important politically, as keeping linkage or common carbon market as an option could gain support from regional and international society when a country wants to establish its own ETS (Ewing and Shin, 2017:8). Both governments and nonprofit organizations have been organizing dialogues on regional market pricing mechanisms to communicate with and learn from each other (Carbon Pulse, 2018).[9]

The second motivation for seeking common ground comes from that learning which can provide opportunity to improve the domestic system. China, Korea, and Japan have learned from pioneers, but they introduced different ETSs to meet their own needs. Fundamental differences between systems have caused fragmentation of regional and international emissions trading markets. Even so, countries continue to learn and communicate, although their purpose may not be to rush to establish a common market. Therefore, it can be pointed out here that all the dialogues and discussions on a more integrated market are probably aimed at overcoming domestic obstacles and continuing to improve the domestic system since these countries are experiencing very different policy practices.

As mentioned in the analytical perspective, learning behaviors of China, Korea, and Japan are not simply limited to mutual learning but also include a process of self-learning. Kay Harrison, a chief markets negotiator for New Zealand, commented on future ETSs that "each market is designed to be appropriate for national circumstances, emphasize the need for nations using market-based approaches to cooperate while encouraging officials to support each other, forge a common understanding and work together on initiatives that might create a convergence that could eventually strengthen the global system" (Carbon Pulse, 2017a). Also, regarding its own domestic carbon markets, Professor Duan Maosheng of Tsinghua University, one of the leading experts in designing China's ETS, said at the COP23 UN climate negotiations in Bonn on December 11, 2017 that "We need to consider the future possibility of linking [when designing the system], but I don't think this is a short-term issue" (Carbon Pulse, 2017a, 2017b). China, Korea, and Japan are exploring many opportunities to enhance communication and cooperation both internationally and domestically, even though it is still too early to argue that the relevant policies and regulations are moving toward harmonization.

To be specific, policy makers have strongly agreed on many occasions that they should continue to learn from others while positively establishing and improving their own ETSs. For instance, an annually and officially organized conference among three countries, "The 3rd Forum of Carbon Pricing Mechanism in Japan, China and Korea" was held in Tokyo on October 22, 2018 by the Institute for Global Environmental Strategies (IGES) with the support of the MOEJ. Participants included the director of the Global Environment Bureau, Mr. Satoru Morishita of MOEJ, the deputy director of the Department of Climate Change, Mr. Feng Liu of the Chinese Ministry of Ecology and Environment (MEE), the director of the Climate Change Mitigation Division, Mr. Jong-Hwan Kim of the Korean Ministry of the Environment. The forum was also attended by researchers as discussants from Waseda University of Japan, Tsinghua University of China, and Kyung Hee University of Korea. Professor Jian-Kun He, who had been serving as an advisor to the Chinese NDRC on ETS, agreed that policy makers in the region should keep learning from each other. Through observing the cooperative behavior of the three countries, maintaining domestic carbon market and economic stability remains one of the most important goals. This is because the close economic ties between the countries give them a strong foundation for possible future integration, but also increase the risks of interdependence. If policy diffusion inevitably leads to policy divergence, the pursuit of policy convergence would not be easy, as it requires careful modeling, simulations, and systems designs over a gradual implementation period through methods such as domestic pilot experimentation to achieve smooth operations in relation to each other's development and progress of ETS while improving domestic schemes.

This cautious attitude echoes the opinions of anti-ETS linkage. There has been some opposition voiced to linking the ETS markets, with claims that the linkages may greatly complicate immature markets, which is also worth noting. Experience has shown that when markets are connected, prices can be easily affected by others, which can cause policy uncertainty and unstable operations (Green, 2017). All in all, these debates highlight the challenges resulting from policy diffusion and fragmentation at both the international and domestic levels, mentioned in Chapter 1 of this volume; that is, because receiving jurisdictions introduce policies and design their own systems based on their own domestic bargaining processes, they face external pressures when addressing the barriers to policy harmonization (Biedenkopf et al., 2017a).

Regardless of the challenges and obstacles highlighted by policy makers, think tanks, and research organizations, at the moment it appears that China, Korea, and Japan are more focused on designing and operating effective domestic carbon markets, which is why this chapter argues that "seeking similarities while keeping the differences" will continue to guide the market integration discussion currently and in the foreseeable future. This is not to say that international cooperation (e.g. policy learning) is no longer going to play an important role in inducing convergence. On the contrary, although there are still many differences and barriers, due to their policy and political learning motivations, the level of actors engaging in knowledge and experience sharing, capacity building, technical and political dialogue, and multilateral coopera-tion across borders is growing (World Bank Group, 2019: 55–8).

5.6   CONCLUSION

This chapter examined the motivations behind, and the process involved in recipient jurisdictions being able to move from policy divergence toward pos-sible harmonization. Through an analysis of the national and sub-national ETS structures, scopes, coverage, and associated policies, ETS developments in the past decade in China, Korea, and Japan were examined and the barriers to and possibility of ETS policy convergence discussed.

Jurisdictions use ETSs as market-based policy tools to achieve reduction targets and tend to establish "real" markets based on economic supply-demand principles through regulations or public guidance to reach their goals (Lederer, 2017: 136). The establishment of northeast Asian ETSs through pilot pro-jects, phased plans, and voluntary schemes has shown that if the purpose and political will is clear and firm, a system can stably operate within its political, economic, industrial, and social contexts. However, because each country is focused on its own domestic needs, there are few commonalities in these regional ETSs.

From a theoretical perspective, discussions on the possibilities of a common ETS market aim to keep a common platform and to deliberate common goals to overcome domestic obstacles. To be specific, there are certain purposes that can motivate cooperation and continuous learning even when the systems are diverse. Firstly, to improve domestic systems, maintaining a common platform allows for self-learning and learning from neighbors and others. Secondly, to reduce risk and uncertainty and enhance mutual confidence, cooperation and continuous communications could lead to development of moderate approaches such as indirect or direct links between markets. All in all, these efforts contribute to achieve common goals and to overcome domestic obstacles; that is, if an integrated market were seen as a favorable option, early and unintermittent engagement at the design and rule-making stage could be beneficial for the relevant jurisdictions.

To fully understand the commonalities and differences, this chapter examined four basic aspects—emissions reduction targets, scope, nature, and coverage—and assessed the difficulties in establishing a common carbon market. It was found that these ETSs had very different scopes, natures, coverage, and compliance in the initial and preparation stages, which indicated that developing a fully integrated regional market could be extremely challenging.

Despite the above, continuous learning has become an approach to address problems faced by countries after diffusion. Empirical studies have revealed strong evidence that despite the difference in basic ETS designs, if countries maintain discussions, share experiences, and enhance cooperation, they will continue to learn. Even though a common market is not yet possible, adopting a "wait-and-see" attitude while stabilizing and improving domestic schemes may create a better environment for future policy convergence.

NOTES

1. A cap-and-trade program is an ETS for controlling carbon emissions and other forms of atmospheric pollution in which an upper limit (cap) is imposed on the total amount of the regulated entities. The cap is allocated to each regulated entity as an "allowance," so that the excess and deficiency of allowance can be traded under the program. The ETSs implemented in the EU, Tokyo, and the northeastern US are cap-and-trade types (Zhou et al., 2018).

2. A workshop on the Chinese national ETS took place in Tokyo on September 21, 2018 with speakers from Tsinghua University and China Beijing Environment Exchange (CBEEX).

3. "As nationally determined contributions to the global response to climate change, all Parties are to undertake and communicate ambitious efforts as defined in Articles 4, 7, 9, 10, 11 and 13 with the view to achieving the purpose of this Agreement as set out in Article 2. The efforts of all Parties will represent a progression over time, while recognizing the need to support developing country

Parties for the effective implementation of this Agreement." The Paris Agreement, UNFCCC.

4. The Intergovernmental Panel on Climate Change (IPCC) defines a "business-as-usual" (BaU) baseline case as the level of emissions that would result if future development trends follow those of the past and no changes in policies take place. See Working Group III: Mitigation, s. 7.3.2.3 Baseline Scenario Concepts. Retrieved from http://www.ipcc.ch/ipccreports/tar/wg3/index.php?idp= 286.

5. Liquidity problems in emissions trading occur when there are low market transactions and there is no aggregate quantitative controlling target to motivate emitters to reduce emissions. From a theoretical perspective, the greater the size of the market and the number of participants, the better the effectiveness and abatement cost reductions; in other words, the more participants, the more they can ensure the liquidity of the market and reduce the low transaction liquidity problems.

6. Japan Federation of Economic Organizations.

7. The author has conducted interviews and fieldwork on ETS in Beijing, Shanghai, and Hubei through 2015 to 2017.

8. A research meeting was organized by the Chinese Environmental Issues Study Group in Tokyo on September 25, 2018, with participation by researchers from Tsinghua University and CBEEX.

9. "The government is backing regular academic meetings with colleagues from China and South Korea to look at the potential for future carbon market links between the three nations" (Carbon Pulse, 2018).

REFERENCES

Asian Development Bank (ADB) (2018a). The Korea emissions trading scheme: Challenges and emerging opportunities. The Asian Development Bank Report, November. Retrieved from https://www.adb.org/publications/korea-emissions -trading-scheme (last assessed December 2018).

Asian Development Bank (ADB) (2018b). Decoding Article 6 of the Paris Agreement. The Asian Development Bank Report, April. Retrieved from https://www.adb.org/ sites/default/files/publication/418831/article6-paris-agreement.pdf (last assessed January 2019).

Asia Society Policy Institute (ASPI) (2018). Business sector action to drive carbon market cooperation in northeast Asia. Asia Society Policy Institute Report and KPMG Samjong, May.

Bang, G., Victor, D.G., and Andresen, S. (2017). California's cap-and-trade system: Diffusion and lessons. *Global Environmental Politics* 17 (3): 12–30, doi: 10.1162/ GLEP_a_00413.

Betsill, M. and Hoffmann, M.J. (2011). The contours of "cap and trade": The evolution of 41 emissions trading systems for greenhouse gases. *Review of Policy Research* 28 (1): 83–106.

Biedenkopf, K., van Eynde, S., and Walker, H. (2017a). Policy infusion through capacity building and project interaction: Greenhouse gas emissions trading in China. *Global Environmental Politics* 17 (3): 91–114, doi: 10.1162/GLEP_a_00417.

Biedenkopf, K., Müller, P., Slominskiand, P., and Wettestad, J. (2017b). A global turn to greenhouse gas emissions trading? Experiments, actors, and diffusion. *Global Environmental Politics* 17 (3): 1–11, doi: 10.1162/GLEP_e_00412.

Busch, P.O., Jörgens, H., and Tews, K. (2005). The global diffusion of regulatory instruments: The making of a new international environmental regime. *The ANNALS of the American Academy of Political and Social Science* 598 (1): 146–67, doi: 10.1177/0002716204272355.

Carbon Pulse (2017a). COP23: ETS links slink back on Asia Pacific countries' priority list, December 13. Retrieved from http://carbon-pulse.com/43335/ (last assessed June 2019).

Carbon Pulse (2017b). China, Japan, Korea carbon market links resurface as talks set for next week, December 16. Retrieved from http://carbon-pulse.com/44890/ (last assessed June 2019).

Carbon Pulse (2018). "Sign of Change"?: Japan's Environment Ministry to draw up carbon pricing proposal, March 19. Retrieved from http://carbon-pulse.com/49198/ (last assessed June 24, 2019).

Central Environment Council Global Environment Subcommittee (2018). On recent circumstances such as the measures against global warming. Ministry of the Environment (MOEJ), January 10. Retrieved from https://www.env.go.jp/press/y060-137/mat05r.pdf (last assessed December 2018).

Cheng, F.T., Kojima, M., Michida, E., and Vogel, D. (2017). Policy diffusion and the fragmentation of environmental regulations in Asian countries. *IDE Research Bulletin*, March.

Daley, D.M. and Garand, J.C. (2005). Horizontal diffusion, vertical diffusion, and internal pressure in state environmental policymaking, 1989–1998. *American Politics Research* 33 (5): 615–44, https://doi.org/10.1177/1532673X04273416.

Dolšak, N. and Sampson, K. (2012). The diffusion of market-based instruments: The case of air pollution. *Administration & Society* 44 (3): 310–42, http://doi.org/10.1177/0095399711400047.

Elkins, Z., Guzman, A.T., and Simmons, B. (2006). Competing for capital: The diffusion of bilateral investment treaties, 1960–2000. *International Organization* 60 (4): 811–46, doi: 10.1017/S0020818306060279.

Ewing, J. (2016). Roadmap to a northeast Asian carbon market. Asian Society Policy Institute Report, December.

Ewing, J. (2017). Building the evidence base for carbon market linkage in northeast Asia. Asian Society Policy Institute White Paper, December 15.

Ewing, J. and Shin, M.-Y. (2017). Northeast Asia and the next generation of carbon market cooperation. Emissions Trading Systems in Northeast Asia Take Center Stage: Asia Society Policy Institute Report, December.

Gilardi, F. (2010). Who learns from what in policy diffusion processes? *American Journal of Political Science* 54 (3): 650–66, doi: 10.1111/j.1540-5907.2010.00452.x.

Gilardi, F. (2012). Transnational diffusion: Norms, ideas, and policies. In C. Walter, T. Risse, and B.A. Simmons (eds), *Handbook of International Relations*. London: Sage, pp. 453–77.

Gilardi, F., Füglister, K., and Stéphane, L. (2009). Learning from others: The diffusion of hospital financing reforms in OECD countries. *Comparative Political Studies* 42 (4): 549–73, doi: 10.1177/0010414008327428.

Green, Jessica F. (2017). Don't link carbon markets. *Nature* 543: 484–6, March 23, doi: 10.1038/543484a.

Gulbrandsen, L., Sammut, F., and Wettestad, J. (2017). Emissions trading and policy diffusion: Complex EU ETS emulation in Kazakhstan. *Global Environmental Politics* 17 (3): 115–33.

Han, G., Olsson, M., Hallding, K., and Lunsford, D. (2012). China's carbon emission trading: An overview of current development. FORES Study 2012:1, FORES, Stockholm, Sweden.

Holzinger, K., Jörgens, H., and Knill, C. (2007). Transfer, diffusion und konvergenz. Konzepte und Kausalmechanismen. In K. Holzinger, H. Jörgens, and C. Knill (eds), *Transfer, Diffusion und Konvergenz von Politiken, PVS— Politische Vierteljahrsschrift*, Sonderheft 38/2007, Wiesbaden: VS Verlag für Sozialwissenschaften, pp. 11–35.

Inderberg, T.H.J., Bailey, I., and Harmer, N. (2017). Designing New Zealand's Emissions Trading Scheme. *Global Environmental Politics* 17(3): 31–50. https://doi.org/10.1162/GLEP_a_00414.

International Carbon Action Partnership (ICAP) (2017). Emissions trading worldwide: Status report 2017. Berlin: ICAP.

International Carbon Action Partnership (ICAP) (2018). Emissions trading worldwide: Status report 2018. Berlin: ICAP.

International Carbon Action Partnership (ICAP) (2020). Emissions trading worldwide: Status report 2020. Berlin: ICAP.

Jörgens, H. (2004). Governance by diffusion—implementing global norms through cross-national imitation and learning. In M.L. William (ed.), *Governance for Sustainable Development: The Challenge of Adapting Form to Function.* Cheltenham, UK and Northampton, MA, USA: Edward Elgar, pp. 246–83.

Kern, K., Jörgens, H., and Jänicke, M. (2005). The diffusion of environmental policy innovations: A contribution to the globalization of environmental policy. WZB Working Paper No. FS II 01-302.

Knox-Hayes, J. (2016). *The Cultures of Markets.* Oxford: Oxford University Press.

Lederer, M. (2017). Carbon pricing: Who gets what, when, and how? *Global Environmental Politics* 17 (3): 134–40, doi: 10.1162/GLEP_a_00419.

Liu, F. (2018). China's national ETS. A 3rd forum of carbon pricing mechanism in Japan, China and Korea, held in Tokyo, October 22.

Lo, A.Y. (2013). Carbon trading in a socialist market economy: Can China make a difference? *Ecological Economics* 87: 72–4, doi: 10.1016/j.ecolecon.2012.12.023.

Lo, A.Y. and Howes, M. (2013). Powered by the state or finance? The organization of China's carbon markets. *Eurasian Geography and Economics* 54 (4): 386–408, doi: 10.1080/15387216.2013.870794.

Mattei, F. (2018). Comparing carbon emission trading schemes of China, Japan and Korea. *Rouse*, September 21.

Meseguer, C. (2005). Policy learning, policy diffusion, and the making of a new order. *The ANNALS of the American Academy of Political and Social Science* 598 (1): 67–82.

Meseguer, C. (2009). *Learning, Policy Making, and Market Reform.* Cambridge: Cambridge University Press.

Ministry of the Environment of Japan (MOEJ) (2016). Cabinet decision on the plan for global warming countermeasures. May 13. Retrieved from https://www.env.go.jp/press/102512.html (last assessed January 2019).

Ministry of Environment of Korea (2018). A 3rd forum of carbon pricing mechanism in Japan, China and Korea, held in Tokyo, October 22.

Müller, P. and Slominski, P. (2016). Theorizing third country agency in EU rule transfer: Linking the EU emissions trading system with Norway, Switzerland and Australia. *Journal of European Public Policy* 23 (6): 814–32, doi: 10.1080/13501763.2015.1066838.

Müller, P. and Slominski, P. (2017). The politics of learning: Developing an emissions trading scheme in Australia. *Global Environmental Politics* 17 (3): 51–68, doi: 10.1162/GLEP_a_00415.

Munnings, C., Morgenstern, R.D., Wang, Z.M., and Liu, X. (2014). Assessing the design of three pilot programs for carbon trading in China. Discussion Paper of Resource for the Future (RFF), October.

Newell, R.G., Pizer, W.A., and Raimi, D. (2013). Carbon markets 15 years after Kyoto: Lessons learned, new challenges. *Journal of Economic Perspectives* 27 (1): 123–46, doi: 10.1257/jep.27.1.123.

Paterson, M., Hoffmann, M., Betsill, M., and Bernstein, S. (2014). The micro foundations of policy diffusion toward complex global governance. *Comparative Political Studies* 47 (3): 420–49, doi: 10.1177/0010414013509575.

Redmond, L. and Convery, F. (2015). The global carbon market-mechanism landscape: Pre and post 2020 perspectives. *Climate Policy* 15 (5): 647–69, doi: 10.1080/14693062.2014.965126.

Schmalensee, R. and Stavins, R. (2013). The SO_2 allowance trading system: The ironic history of a grand policy experiment. *Journal of Economic Perspectives* 27 (1): 103–22, doi: 10.3386/w18306.

Shipan, C.R. and Volden, C. (2008). The mechanisms of policy diffusion. *American Journal of Political Science* 52 (4): 840–57, doi: 10.1111/j.1540-5907.2008.00346.x.

Skjærseth, J.B. and Wettestad, J. (2008). *EU Emissions Trading—Initiation, Decision-making and Implementation.* Aldershot, UK: Ashgate.

Tews, K. and Busch, P.-O. (2001). Governance by diffusion? Potentials and restrictions of environmental policy diffusion. *Proceedings of the 2001 Berlin Conference*, Potsdam, pp. 168–82.

Tews, K., Busch P.-O., and Jörgens, H. (2003). The diffusion of new environmental policy instruments. *European Journal of Political Research* 42 (4): 569–600, doi: 10.1111/1475-6765.00096.

The Paris Agreement (2015). UNFCCC. Retrieved from https://unfccc.int/sites/default/files/english_paris_agreement.pdf (last assessed November 2018).

Underdal, A. (2013). Meeting common environmental challenges: The co-evolution of policies and practices. *International Environmental Agreements* 13 (1): 15–30, doi: 10.1007/s10784-012-9203-0.

Underdal, A., Victor D.G., and Wettestad, J. (2015). Studying the global diffusion of emissions trading: Key building blocks in the ETS-DIFFUSION Project Research Design. FNI Report 2/2015. Fridtjof Nansen Institute, Lysaker, Norway.

Wettestad, J. and Gulbrandsen, L.H. (eds) (2017). *The Evolution of Carbon Markets: Design and Diffusion.* London: Routledge.

World Bank (2016). Exploring east Asian cooperation on carbon markets, June 16. Retrieved from http://www.worldbank.org/en/news/feature/2016/06/16/exploring-east-asian-cooperation-on-carbon-markets (last assessed January 2019).

World Bank Group (2019). State and Trends of Carbon Pricing 2019. Washington, DC: World Bank. Retrieved from https://openknowledge.worldbank.org/handle/10986/31755 (last assessed June 2019).

Xiong, L. and Qi, S.-Z. (2015). Carbon trading market in China: Present situation and prospect. In W.-G. Wang and G.-G. Zheng (eds), *Annual Report on Actions to Address Climate Change 2015: A New Start and Hope in Paris.* Beijing: Social Science Academic Press, pp. 187–201.

Zhou, W.-S., Hu, Y., Qian, X.-P., and Nakagami, K. (2018). Design for east Asia emission trading scheme (EA-ETS): From European Union to Japan-China-South Korea linking. *Policy Science* 25 (3): 251–71, doi: 10.34382/00005230.

6. The diffusion of energy efficiency policies in Asian countries: country-specific drivers of policy followers

Michikazu Kojima

6.1   INTRODUCTION

Environmental policy diffusion has been a topic of interest in the social sciences, especially political science and sociology. Gilardi (2013) reviewed the transnational diffusion of policies and pointed out an emerging consensus regarding the mechanisms of policy diffusion, which can be grouped into four broad categories: coercion, competition, learning, and emulation.

Although many studies have proposed mechanisms that are common across the globe, some studies have focused on country-specific factors. Beise (2004) identified country-specific factors that determined global leaders in innovation diffusion, such as advantages in demand, exporting, information transfer, and market structure. Beise and Rennings (2005) discussed the types of regulations and other factors that affected diffusion of innovation. These two studies, though dedicated specifically to innovation diffusion, imply that policy diffusion should also be affected by country-specific factors. Jänikcke (2005) studied the character and role of trend setters or pioneers in environmental policy, finding that the main factors determining a country's pioneering role included the general strength of its green advocacy coalition and its opportunity structure, both of which are country-specific. Shipan and Volden (2008) discussed the impact of domestic forces and outside actors, such as other jurisdictions and international organizations, on policy diffusion.

To mitigate urgent global environmental problems such as climate change, various policies should be diffused faster and more effectively. The timing of policy adoption by followers should be studied as a means of understanding ways to accelerate policy diffusion.

Since improvements in energy efficiency can contribute to the mitigation of climate change, this area of environmental policy deserves careful study.

Lovins (1977) highlighted the importance of energy efficiency and criticized government energy policies that focused only on the supply of conventional energy sources, such as oil, coal, and nuclear power. He also stressed the importance of a decentralized energy supply system. It is possible to diffuse energy efficient technology without government intervention, because improving energy efficiency is beneficial. However, Okazaki and Yamaguchi (2011), who examined policy barriers to the implementation of energy-saving technologies by the steel industry, identified two government-related obstacles along with economic and technological barriers. The first of these was the lack of efficiency standards or incentives provided by national policy; the second was inadequate technical guidelines and assistance. Adopting efficiency policy is important, even if there is the possibility to diffuse energy efficiency technologies without government intervention.

The present chapter seeks to identify the country-specific drivers of followers in the realm of Asian energy efficiency policy. The United States became a pioneer in this field by enacting the Energy Policy and Conservation Act in December 1975. This act included energy conservation measures, such as reasonable restrictions on the public or private use of energy, and energy efficiency measures, including provisions governing automobile fuel economy, energy efficiency standards for consumer products, industrial energy efficiency improvement targets, and energy efficiency standards for buildings.

Some Asian countries, such as Japan and South Korea, introduced energy conservation policies around 1980, patterned on the US policy. However, most Asian countries did not establish similar policies governing energy efficiency until after 1992. This chapter also identifies the international political and economic circumstances that have affected energy efficiency policy in Asian countries over the different time periods.

The chapter is structured as follows. Section 6.2 introduces the types of policies used to improve energy efficiency. Section 6.3 describes the diffusion of energy efficiency policies in selected Asian countries. Section 6.4 summarizes common country-specific drivers of the introduction of energy efficiency policies during four time periods: around 1980, from 1983 to 1989, from 1990 to 2005, and after 2005. Finally, Section 6.5 discusses the findings of this chapter, compared with previous studies.

6.2   TYPES OF ENERGY EFFICIENCY POLICIES

The various types of energy efficiency policies can be categorized by sector, such as those governing factories, transportation, buildings, machines and appliances, and general measures (Table 6.1).

Table 6.1   Types of energy efficiency policy

Sector	Policy
Factory	Energy Manager
	Energy Management Plan
	Energy Audit
Transportation	Modal shift
	Improve transportation efficiency (increase loading rate, shorten the route of transportation)
	Reduce the distance for forwarding
Building	Prevention of heat loss through outer wall and window
	Efficient use of air conditioning
	Efficient use of lighting
	Efficient use of hot water supply system
	Efficient use of elevator
Machines,	Minimum Energy Performance Standards (MEPS)
Appliances	Energy efficiency labeling
General Measures	Financial incentives for above policies such as subsidy and tax
	Legal requirement

Source: Compiled by the author from various sources.

Factories are responsible for a large portion of energy use. The power generation, steel, non-ferrous metal, chemical, cement, and pulp and paper industries are particularly energy-intensive. Because of the wide range of industrial processes, it is very difficult to set broadly applicable energy efficiency standards. Policies to improve energy efficiency in factories generally require companies to appoint an energy manager, conduct energy audits, and develop and implement an energy management plan.

In the transportation sector, a modal shift encouraging more energy-efficient modes of transportation, such as ships and train, has been promoted. Improving transportation efficiency by increasing the loading rate and shortening transportation routes is also important.

Buildings use large amounts of energy for lighting, air conditioning, hot water supply, elevators, and other purposes. Installation of energy-efficient equipment in buildings can significantly reduce consumption. Energy use for air conditioning can be reduced by improving building insulation to prevent heat loss. Building design should take energy efficiency concerns into account. Accordingly, energy efficiency regulations may require changes in building design and energy management planning.

Improving the energy efficiency of equipment, such as automobiles, refrigerators, and air conditioners, can also contribute to energy savings. The establishment of minimum energy performance standards can eliminate energy-inefficient equipment from the market. Product labeling can help environmentally sensitive consumers to take energy efficiency into account when they buy products.

Finally, general measures, including financial incentives (such as taxes and subsidies) and other legal requirements, can also be applied in all the above-mentioned sectors.

These measures have usually not all been introduced at once; many countries have adopted them gradually and in different chronological order. Each country has had its own priorities with regard to the initiation of policy measures intended to improve energy efficiency.

6.3   THE ESTABLISHMENT OF ENERGY EFFICIENCY REGULATIONS IN SELECTED ASIAN COUNTRIES

6.3.1   Japan

Japan enacted the Act Concerning the Rational Use of Energy in 1979, with the purpose of improving energy efficiency in factories, buildings, and machinery. Factories that consumed more than 3000 kl of oil equivalent or 12 million kWh of electricity annually were required to appoint an energy manager and record energy use.

In 1993, this act was revised to require factories covered by its provisions to report their energy use to the government. In 1998, the act was revised again; this time, the major change was the introduction of a "top-runner approach" to set the standard of machinery. Producers must meet a certain standard in terms of the average energy efficiency of products sold in the market during a year. The standard is set by taking into account the "top runner," that is, the most energy-efficient equipment in a reference year. The producer is expected to meet this standard within a few years. The government stipulates the specific time frame, 4–6 years, to satisfy the standard. The 1998 amendments also required medium-sized factories to appoint an energy management officer.

These efforts in Japan have been highlighted by researchers in other countries. For example, Lu et al. (2008) compared the energy efficiency policies in Japan with those in other developed countries such as Germany, the United States (specifically the state of California), and the United Kingdom, concluding that Japan's efforts to improve energy efficiency were the most successful.

6.3.2   South Korea

South Korea adopted the Energy Use Rationalization Act in 1979, and the Korea Energy Management Corporation (KEMCO) was established in 1980 based on this act. KEMCO promotes energy audits, training and information services, and inspections and sets specifications for some energy-using equipment. KEMCO also manages a fund for low-interest loans to finance various energy management projects, including efficiency investments and better home insulation (IEA, 1992).

The International Energy Agency (1994) reviewed South Korea's energy efficiency program in the early 1990s, finding that energy efficiency had improved from 1970 to 1985 but then declined from 1985 to 1991.

Standards and labeling requirements for equipment were initiated in the 1980s, based on the Energy Use Rationalization Act, but rank-based ratings were not implemented at that time. Energy efficiency standards and additional labeling programs were launched in 1992. Initially, an endorsement-type labeling approach was applied. However, after the International Energy Agency (1994) called for the use of rating labels, South Korea subsequently implemented this change. The labeling program now covers 37 appliances, including home appliances, lighting products, vehicles, and tires. A high-efficiency equipment certification program was started in 1996, covering 45 items including pumps, boilers, and LED lights (MOTIE and Korea Energy Agency, 2015).

The Energy Use Rationalization Act was revised in 2002, 2003, and 2008. Measures to improve energy efficiency have been added in these revisions.

6.3.3   Taiwan

Taiwan enacted and implemented its Energy Management Act in 1980, thereby defining the responsibilities of stakeholders in energy efficiency. The Energy Commission of the Ministry of Economic Affairs began setting up energy efficiency standards for various products in 1981 (APEC, 1994).

Taiwan's government developed an executive master plan for energy conservation policy in 2005. However, political struggles deterred the implementation of this master plan. Lu et al. (2008) also pointed out that low electricity prices reduced incentives to improve energy efficiency, as politicians were afraid to lose popular support by imposing stiffer energy restrictions.

6.3.4   The Philippines

The Philippines enacted the Omnibus Energy Conservation Act in 1980. The Ministry of Energy (1980) hosted training courses on energy conservation for industry personnel (Ministry of Energy, 1980). According to the Ministry of Energy (1984), more than 1800 energy managers were trained.

In 1992, Republic Act No. 7638 (An Act Creating the Department of Energy Rationalizing the Organization and Functions of Government Agencies Related to Energy and for Other Purposes) established an Energy Utilization

Management Bureau in the Department of Energy. This bureau is responsible for various activities related to energy efficiency, such as energy audits, energy management advisory services, and nationwide campaigns.

6.3.5   Thailand

Thailand depended heavily on external energy resources in the 1970s. The country's energy self-reliance rate was only 51.8% in 1980 (ADB, 1992). A 1980 country paper on Thailand by the United Nations Economic and Social Commission for Asia and the Pacific (ESCAP) explained how an individual company had reduced heat loss from its steam supply, but it made no mention of policies on energy efficiency. To mitigate the impact of a surge in oil prices in the 1970s, Thailand put more effort into exploiting domestic energy resources, such as oil production, rather than into demand-side management of energy.

Around 1990, Thailand began to focus on energy efficiency. The International Institute of Energy Conservation estimated in 1990 that demand-side management could reduce peak electricity demand by 2000 MW by 2000. This study stimulated work on a comprehensive demand-side management plan, which received government approval in 1991 (World Bank, 1993). The importance of demand-side energy management was also stressed in Thailand's report to the United Nations Conference on Environment and Development, held in Rio de Janeiro, Brazil, in June 1992.

In 1992, Thailand enacted the Energy Conservation Act, which identified the lead implementation agency for energy conservation, directed this authority to set voluntary appliance energy standards, and required "controlled facilities," such as large factories, to appoint an energy manager and develop an energy conservation plan, among other provisions. Thailand obtained international cooperation from the World Bank and other donors in these efforts (World Bank, 2006).

The Thailand Promotion of Electricity Energy Efficiency project, which was approved by the Global Environmental Facility (GEF), supported the Electricity Generating Authority of Thailand (EGAT) in conducting a demand-side management program. EGAT instituted energy performance labeling and promoted an energy-efficient fluorescent lamp.

6.3.6   China

In 1986, China enacted Provisional Regulations on the Control of Energy Conservation. These provisional regulations focused on enterprises that consumed more than 10,000 tons per year of standard coal, stipulating that such enterprises should appoint an energy manager.

China received international cooperation on energy efficiency matters from the GEF and other donors after 1995. The China Efficient Industrial Boilers project, approved by the GEF council in 1996, developed affordable energy-efficient industrial boiler designs, which were produced and sold in the Chinese market. Chinese manufacturers also obtained assistance in designing and producing efficient chlorofluorocarbon-free refrigerators, which were approved in 1998 by the GEF council.

In 1997, China enacted the Law on Energy Conservation, which took effect on January 1, 1998. This law included sections on energy audits and management and on labeling requirements for energy-using products, among other topics.

Initiatives to improve energy efficiency in China have accelerated since 2004, when the National Development and Reform Commission issued its Medium and Long-term Plan for Energy Conservation (Zhou et al., 2010). The National Energy Efficiency Standard for Public Buildings was enacted by the Ministry of Housing and Urban-Rural Development in 2005.

With regard to the industry sector, China started to focus on its top 1000 energy-consuming enterprises in 2006. These enterprises are now subjected to energy audits and must submit energy audit reports to the provincial government. They must also develop an energy conservation plan annually.

At the National Teleconference on Energy Conservation and Emissions Reduction in 2007, Chinese Prime Minister Wen Jibao criticized the rapid growth of energy-intensive industries that generated large amounts of pollutants. Energy conservation efforts were strengthened, and the Law on Energy Conservation was revised in 2008 (Yergin, 2011).

China introduced a top-runner endorsement for refrigerators, air conditioners with inverters, and flat-panel televisions in 2015. If a product achieves the highest level of energy efficiency, it can be advertised as a "top runner." This approach differs from the Japanese top-runner system, which requires all manufacturers to achieve a certain energy efficiency level, as determined by the most energy-efficient product in a reference year, over a stipulated time period (Ministry of Economy, Trade and Industry, 2015).

6.3.7   India

Various initiatives to improve energy efficiency occurred in India before 1980. A country paper by ESCAP (1980) described existing initiatives to improve energy efficiency. More efficient stoves using wood and other non-commercial fuels had been developed. A project aimed at energy conservation in public and government buildings had been conducted by the Central Building Research Institute, sponsored by the Ministry of Energy.

In 1989, the Energy Management Center was established as an autonomous organization, with support from the World Bank and United Nations Development Programme. In 2001, India enacted its Energy Conservation Act, on the basis of which the Bureau of Energy Efficiency was established in 2002. The act also required that factories of a certain size in 15 industries, such as cement, fertilizer, and steel, must appoint an energy manager, conduct energy audits, submit a three-year plan for implementing financially viable measures, and report energy use to the government. The Electricity Act of 2003 also emphasized the efficient use of electricity. This measure prompted the formulation of the National Electricity Plan, which highlighted demand-side management.

India's Energy Conservation Building Code was established in 2007. A few states made compliance with the Code mandatory, but most states treated it as voluntary. In 2017, the Energy Conservation Building Code was amended and became mandatory throughout the country.

The National Action Plan for Climate Change (NAPCC) was launched in mid-2010. One of the eight missions contained in the NAPCC was the National Mission of Enhanced Energy Efficiency, which included such initiatives as enhancing the energy efficiency of power plants and promoting energy-efficient appliances and machinery (Vasudevan et al., 2011).

6.3.8   Indonesia

Indonesia carried out a public campaign, training, and education to encourage the rational and efficient use of energy in 1979 (IEA, 1993). Presidential instruction on the road map for energy conservation was issued in 1982, and a Master Plan on Energy Conservation was formulated in 1985. In 1992, a National Energy Conservation Campaign took place. However, no regulations resulted from this activity.

In 2007, Indonesia adopted its Law of Energy, Article 25 of which placed responsibility for energy conservation on national and regional governments, business entities, and the people. However, the law did not mention any policy measures related to energy efficiency.

Indonesia's most detailed policy on energy conservation is defined in Government Regulation No. 70/2009 on Energy Conservation. Under this regulation, major energy consumers that consume more than 6000 equivalent tons of oil per annum must undertake energy management, including appointment of an energy manager, formulation of an energy conservation program, and implementation of an energy audit. Labeling standards are also mentioned in Article 15 of the government regulation.

6.3.9 Malaysia

A Malaysia country paper by ESCAP (1980) indicated that performance stand-ards and control services for heating and cooling systems in households and offices were being introduced. Furthermore, the paper mentioned that financial aid and tax credits were available for activities to improve energy efficiency in industries. Malaysia created a National Energy Efficiency Program in 1991, and in 1998 the Malaysia Energy Center, which has conducted various pro-grams to improve energy efficiency, was established.

However, not until 2008 were regulations to promote energy efficiency enacted (as the Efficient Management of Electrical Energy Regulations Act). A 2013 revision of electricity regulations, originally adopted in 1994, intro-duced energy labeling on some home appliances.

6.3.10 Vietnam

Prime Minister Decision on approving the national target program of econom-ical and efficient use of energy was issued in April 2006. The decision iden-tified the key areas to improve energy efficiency, such as awareness raising, setting standard for energy-use products, construction of buildings, and others. It also stated that legal documents such as laws and sub-laws would be devel-oped between 2006 and 2010.

In 2010, Vietnam enacted its Law on Economical and Efficient Use of Energy, which took effect on January 1, 2011. The law covered various meas-ures to improve energy efficiency, such as energy labeling, financial support, energy management plans by industries, and energy managers. The Australian government supported such activities from June 2012 to August 2015 through the Vietnam Energy Efficiency Standards and Labelling program (Michaells, 2015). In 2017, the World Bank started "Vietnam Energy Efficiency for Industrial Enterprises" project. The major component of the project is energy efficiency investment lending.

6.3.11 Singapore

A country paper on Singapore by the Economic and Social Commission for Asia and Pacific (ESCAP, 1980) mentioned efficiency improvements in the power sector but did not mention the demand-side management of energy use. In 2008, Singapore introduced mandatory energy efficiency requirements for large buildings, mandatory labeling, and minimum energy performance standards.

Singapore then enacted its Energy Conservation Act in 2012 as part of its activities to reduce greenhouse gas (GHG) emissions. The design of energy efficiency labeling for air conditioners, refrigerators, and clothes dryers was revised in 2014. It required that the information on estimated annual energy cost in use should be mentioned in the label.

6.4   COUNTRY-SPECIFIC FACTORS UNDERLYING DIFFUSION AND NON-DIFFUSION

The main country-specific drivers contributing to the diffusion of energy efficiency policies around 1980 differed from those after the 1990s. Table 6.2 shows the year of the adoption of major energy efficiency regulations in 11 Asian countries or regions and the United States. The table displays a chronological gap. Around 1980, the first four countries (Japan, South Korea, Taiwan, and the Philippines) enacted energy efficiency regulation, but other Asian countries did not join in this trend until after 1992. This section summarizes the country-specific forces driving diffusion in four time periods: around 1980, the mid-1980s to 1989, 1990 to 2005, and after 2005.

Table 6.2   Acts on energy efficiency in Asia

	Year	Regulation
US	1975	Energy Policy and Conservation Act
Japan	1979	Law on Rational Use of Energy
South Korea	1979	Energy Utilization Act
Taiwan	1980	Energy Management Act
Philippines	1980	Omnibus Energy Conservation Act in 1980
Thailand	1992	Energy Conservation Promotion Act. B.E.2535
China	1997	Energy Conservation Law of China
India	2001	Energy Conservation Act
Malaysia	2008	Efficient Management of Electrical Energy Regulations
Indonesia	2009	Government Regulation No. 70 Year 2009 on Energy Conservation
Vietnam	2010	Law on Economical and Efficient Use of Energy
Singapore	2012	Energy Conservation Act

Source: Compiled from various sources.

6.4.1   Factors Underlying Diffusion and Non-diffusion around 1980

When Japan, South Korea, Taiwan, and the Philippines introduced energy efficiency regulations around 1980, these countries closely followed the United States, which had adopted an energy conservation policy in 1975.

In October 1973, the Arab–Israeli war started and oil-producing Arab countries implemented an embargo on oil shipments to the United States, the Netherlands, Portugal, Rhodesia, and South Africa. They also reduced production to apply political pressure on unfriendly states. The price of oil and other energy resources increased sharply. The US energy conservation policy represented a response to this situation.

The four early actors in Asian energy conservation policy all had close relationships with the United States. Their policy actions around 1980 were triggered by another hike in oil prices due to the Iranian Revolution, which reduced Iran's oil production.

Figure 6.1 shows energy intensity and self-reliance in commercial energy consumption in several Asian countries. Where energy intensity is high, there is room to improve energy efficiency; also, high energy prices may have greater economic impact in countries with high energy intensity. As a result, such countries have a particularly strong incentive to improve energy efficiency.

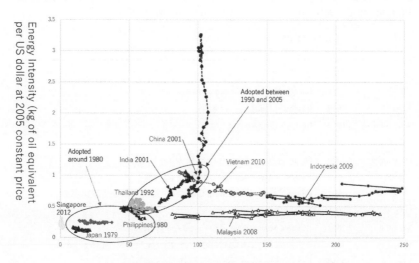

Self-Reliance Rate in Energy Consumption (%)

Figure 6.1   *Energy Intensity, Self-Reliance in Energy Consumption and Year of Adoption of Energy Efficiency Policy*

Note: Following the country name is the year the law on energy efficiency was enacted.
Source: Compiled by the author, based on the World Development Indicators.

Self-reliance in energy consumption is determined by the relative contribution of domestic energy resource extraction to total energy consumption. A self-reliance percentage greater than 100% indicates that the country is a net exporter of energy. If the national government can control domestic energy prices, a country with high self-reliance may have little incentive to adopt energy efficiency policy.

These two factors—high energy efficiency and self-reliance—explain why China did not enact an energy efficiency policy during this period.

Thailand had a slightly lower level of self-reliance in commercial energy consumption than the Philippines. However, Thailand put greater effort into increasing its domestic energy supply than into improving energy efficiency. Its self-reliance rate increased by 11.5 percentage points during the 1980s.

The data of Taiwan are not available in the same source. But the Asian Development Bank (1992) indicates that energy intensity in gross domestic product (GDP) is almost the same as that of South Korea. Regarding Singapore, self-reliance on energy consumption was 0% in 1980. In addition, the level of energy intensity was between that of South Korea and Japan. But Singapore became a center of oil refinery in the region. Some oil refinery plants were developed by major petrochemical companies such as Shell, Mobil, British Petroleum, and Esso, from 1961 to 1971.[1] So Singapore did not need to adopt an energy efficiency policy.

The learning mechanism worked in Japan, South Korea, Taiwan, and the Philippines in this period. In addition, the close diplomatic relationship between these countries and the United States was an important factor. US allies were under pressure from oil-producing countries in the Middle East. The diplomatic relationship with the United States combined with pressure from oil-producing countries may be seen as indirect coercion to adopt energy efficiency policy. To remain allies with the United States, these countries aimed to improve energy efficiency.

6.4.2   The Mid-1980s to 1989

The monthly average price of oil peaked in November 1980, at 40.97 US dollars per barrel, and decreased gradually after that. From February 1986 to December 1989, the monthly average oil price did not exceed 20 US dollars (Figure 6.2).

During this period, most Asian countries did not take substantial action to improve energy efficiency. China was the only exception, introducing its Provisional Regulations on the Control of Energy Conservation. But these regulations focused only on large enterprises and did not comprehensively address energy efficiency in various sectors. The low price of oil can be considered the major factor explaining the inaction on energy efficiency in Asian countries from the mid-1980s to 1989.

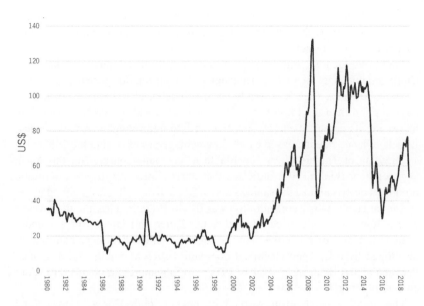

Figure 6.2   Oil Price from 1980s (Unit: US dollar)

Source: International Monetary Fund "Commodity Price."

6.4.3   1990 to 2005

In the 1990s, oil prices were generally lower than those around 1979, when the Iranian Revolution produced the second oil shock of the 1970s. However, two countries, namely Thailand and China, introduced regulations concerning energy efficiency. The enactment of these regulations resulted from growing international attention to climate change, which began to attract wide public and political attention around 1990.

In 1988, the International Panel on Climate Change (IPCC) was established. The IPCC published its first report in 1990. The United Nations Framework Convention on Climate Change was adopted in 1992 and entered into force in 1994. The GEF, an international financial mechanism managed by the World Bank and designed to support developing countries in addressing global environmental issues, was established in 1991. Energy efficiency improvement programs were regarded as a measure to mitigate climate change.

In Asia, Thailand, China, and the Philippines obtained support for energy efficiency programs from the GEF and other donors during the 1990s (Birner and Martinot, 2005). As noted above, Thailand and China enacted laws on energy conservation during the 1990s. The Philippines also reintroduced an energy efficiency program by creating the Energy Utilization Management Bureau in its Department of Energy.

The Kyoto Protocol in 1997 compelled developed countries to reduce GHG emissions. In Asia, only Japan and Turkey were classified as Annex I countries with an obligation to cut GHGs. Japan fully revised its Law on Rational Use of Energy and introduced a top-runner approach to setting energy efficiency requirements for producers of home appliances and automobiles. In addition, large office buildings were required to implement an energy management program. Severe GHG reduction targets contained in the Kyoto Protocol forced Japan to develop stricter energy efficiency regulations.

Other Asian countries also developed measures to improve energy efficiency. India established its Energy Conservation Act in 2001 and gained international support for energy efficiency measures.

After no policy diffusion from the mid-1980s to 1990, circumstances changed in the 1990s due to the increased attention devoted to climate change and the initiation of international cooperative efforts to mitigate this threat. Countries that received international assistance related to improving energy efficiency established various regulations. China, India, and Thailand generated relatively higher CO_2 emission per GDP (Figure 6.3). The learning mechanism of policy diffusion worked well in this period.

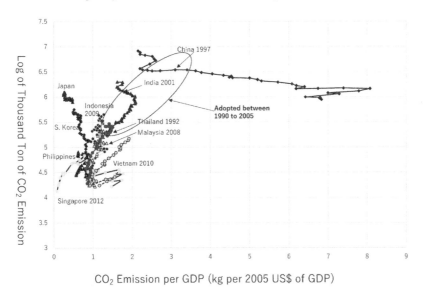

Figure 6.3 CO_2 *Emission and Year of Adoption of Energy Efficiency Policy*

Note: Following the country name is the year the law on energy efficiency was enacted.
Source: Compiled by the author, based on the World Development Indicators.

However, countries having abundant energy resources, such as Malaysia and Indonesia, did not adopt an energy efficiency policy. Singapore, which does not have energy resources, also did not adopt an energy efficiency policy in this period because it was a center of oil refineries.

It should be also noted that the competition mechanism works in applying the top-runner approach to the energy efficiency program. The top-runner approach focuses innovation in the highest energy efficiency products, while a conventional energy efficiency program focuses on the minimum standard. Although the way in which the top-runner approach applied is different, China follows the concept of the Japanese top-runner program.

6.4.4   After 2005

Since 2005, other Asian countries have joined the trend of introducing energy efficiency regulations, including Malaysia in 2007, Indonesia in 2009, Vietnam in 2010, and Singapore in 2013.

In addition to growing international cooperation, an increase in energy prices also impacted efforts in these countries. In August 2004, the monthly average oil price exceeded its November 1980 level. In July 2008, oil hit $132 per barrel in US dollars. This high energy price promoted the introduction of energy efficiency regulations in Asian countries.

International discourse subsequent to the Kyoto Protocol also likely had an impact on these countries' enactment of energy efficiency regulations. Negotiations on the framework of post-Kyoto Protocol mechanisms began in 2005. In 2007, the Bali Action Plan, which stated that developing countries should also take actions to mitigate climate change, was adopted.

These circumstances prompted energy-rich countries, such as Indonesia and Malaysia, to enact energy efficiency regulations. Learning and a weak coercion mechanism through the Kyoto Protocol and Bali Action Plan worked in Indonesia, Malaysia, Vietnam, and Singapore.

Around 1980, domestic factors such as low self-reliance and high energy intensity were the major country-specific drivers to enact energy efficiency regulations in the context of high oil prices. Japan, South Korea, Taiwan, and the Philippines followed the US energy conservation policy. The diffusion of energy efficiency policy slowed from the mid-1980s to 1990, as oil prices were so low as to discourage investment in improving energy efficiency. Four mechanisms of policy diffusion, learning, coercion, and competition, are present in the diffusion of energy efficiency policy in these 40 years.

6.5   CONCLUSION

Asian countries have adopted energy efficiency policies. A comparison of the characteristics of countries at the time they adopted such policies reveals that the country-specific factors affecting their actions are the self-reliance rate in energy consumption, energy intensity, and cooperation from the donor.

This review also shows that the learning mechanism contributes to diffusion of energy efficiency policy. In addition, the timing in adopting the policy is affected not only by country-specific factors, but also the international circumstances such as international relations, oil prices, and the emerging international regime on climate change.

Cooperation in policy formulation and capacity development in developing countries are important in accelerating the adoption of an energy efficiency policy. Many governments of developing countries have difficulties in formulating policies, raising awareness, and raising capacity for implementing new policies. From the viewpoint of donor agencies and improving the effectiveness of international cooperation, target countries for international cooperation should be selected by examining country-specific factors affecting adoption and implementation of new policies.

NOTE

1.   Websites on the history of Singapore hosted by the Singapore government. "Shell Opens Singapore's First Oil Refinery at Pula Bukom, 26th July 1961" (http://eresources.nlb.gov.sg/history/events/37c6a7dd-c7de-4378-819e-e2407839f8d5) and "ESSO's Refinery Opens at Pulau Ayer Chawan, 19 February 1971" (last accessed January 19, 2018) and http://eresources.nlb.gov.sg/history/events/5e547f82-ef3b-489b-8a2a-79ece9f14cea   (last accessed January 19, 2018).

REFERENCES

Asian Development Bank (ADB) (1992). *Energy Indicators of Developing Member Countries of ADB*, Manila.

Asia-Pacific Economic Cooperation (APEC) (1994). *Compendium of Energy Efficiency and Conservation Policies/Programs, Regulations and Standards*, Oak Ridge.

Beise, M. (2004). Lead markets: Country-specific drivers of the global diffusion of innovations. *Research Policy*, 33, 997–1018, doi:10.1016/j.respol.2004.03.003.

Beise, M. and Rennings, K. (2005). Lead markets and regulation: A framework for analyzing the international diffusion of environmental innovations. *Ecological Economics*, 52, 5–17, doi:10.1016/j.ecolecon.2004.06.007.

Birner, S. and Martinot, E. (2005). Promoting energy-efficient products: GEF experience and lessons for market transformation in developing countries. *Energy Policy*, 33, 1765–79, doi:10.1016/j.enpol.2004.01.015.

Economic and Social Commission for Asia and Pacific (ESCAP) (1980). *Proceedings of the Working Group Meeting on Efficiency and Conservation in the Use of Energy*, Bangkok.

Gilardi, F. (2013). Transnational diffusion: Norms, ideas and policies. In E. Carlsnaes, T. Risse and B.A. Simmons (eds), *Handbook of International Relations*, London: Sage, pp. 453–77.

International Energy Agency (IEA) (1992). *Energy Policies of the Republic of Korea*, Paris.

International Energy Agency (IEA) (1993). *International Conference on Energy Efficiency in Asian Countries*, Paris.

International Energy Agency (IEA) (1994). *Energy Policies of the Republic of Korea: 1994 Survey*, Paris.

Jänikcke, Martin (2005). Trend-setters in environmental policy: The character and role of pioneer countries. *Environmental Policy and Governance*, 15(2), 129–42.

Lovins, A. (1977). *Soft Energy Paths: Towards a Durable Peace*. Cambridge: Friends of the Earth International.

Lu, S.M., Huan, Y.S. and Lu, J.M. (2008). Planning an energy-conserving policy for Taiwan based on international examples of success. *Energy Policy*, 36(7), 2685–93, doi:10.1016/j.enpol.2008.03.033.

Michaells, C. (2015). *Vietnam energy efficiency standards and labelling programme evaluation.* Report prepared for the Australian Government, Department of Industry and Science.

Ministry of Economy, Trade and Industry (2015). *Top runner program: Developing the world's best energy-efficient appliances and more*, Japan. Retrieved from http://www.enecho.meti.go.jp/category/saving_and_new/saving/data/toprunner2015e.pdf (last accessed June 2019).

Ministry of Energy (1980). *Five-year energy program 1981–85*, Manila, Philippines.

Ministry of Energy (1984). *Accomplishment report: Energy self-reliance 1973–1983*, Manila, Philippines.

Ministry of Trade, Industry and Economy (MOTIE) and Korea Energy Agency (2015). *Korea energy efficiency policies: Korea's standard & labeling.*

Okazaki, T. and Yamaguchi, M. (2011). Accelerating the transfer and diffusion of energy saving technologies steel sector experience—lessons learned. *Energy Policy*, 39(3), 1296–304, doi:10.1016/j.enpol.2010.12.001.

Shipan, C.R. and Volden, C. (2008). The mechanism of policy diffusion. *American Journal of Political Studies*, 52(4), 840–57.

Vasudevan, R., Cherail, K., Bhatia, R. and Jayaram, N. (2011). *Energy efficiency in India: History and Overview*. New Delhi: Alliance for an Energy Efficient Economy. Retrieved from https://aeee.in/wp-content/uploads/2016/03/AEEE-EE-Book-Online-Version-.pdf (last accessed November 2020).

World Bank (1993). *Thailand: Promotion of Electricity Energy Efficiency Project*, Project Document, Washington, DC.

World Bank (2006). *Thailand: Promotion of Electrical Energy Efficiency Project, World Bank GEF Post-implementation Impact Assessment*, Washington, DC.

Yergin, Daniel (2011). *The Quest: Energy Security, and the Remaking of the Modern World*, New York: Penguin Books.

Zhou, N., Levine, M.D. and Price L. (2010). Overview of current energy efficiency policies in China. *Energy Policy*, 38(11), 6439–452, doi:10.1016/j.enpol.2009.08.015.

Index